The Best of Epicure's

NOUVELLE INDIAN CUISINE

Asha Khatau

Popular Prakashan
www.popularprakashan.com

Published by
Harsha Bhatkal for
POPULAR PRAKASHAN PVT. LTD.
301, Mahalaxmi Chambers
22, Bhulabhai Desai Road
Mumbai – 400 026
www.popularprakashan.com

First Published 2017

(4466)

ISBN: 978-81-7991-907-1

Photography: Mangesh Parab
Design: Anjali Sawant

Printed in India
by Saurabh Printers (P) Ltd.
Plot No. 67 A-68, Ecotech, Ext. I
Kasna, Greater Noida-201306 (U.P)

Dedication

I dedicate this book to my sister, Hina Bhatia, (Late) Bina Tejpal and Raksha Patel.

Acknowledgements

To the One above, for making me so strong and capable.

The making of *Nouvelle Indian Cuisine*, the latest book in The Best of Epicure series, happened with the constant support, encouragement and help of many people whom I wish to thank.

Firstly, my heartfelt thanks to my immediate family i.e. my mother-in-law Leela Khatau for giving me encouragement and support in all I do. I remember my late mother Sudha Sampat for giving me inspiration and courage while alive. I sincerely thank my husband Mahendra Khatau for his constructive suggestions and moral support. Help from my three children, Priya, Shreya and Manish does not go unnoticed. I thank them from my heart. My special thanks to Abhaji Singhania for her help and expert's touch during the photo shoot. I would also like to thank my friends Vandana Kejriwal and Niti Desai for helping during the photoshoot. I want to thank my cooking class students, Bindal, Shrepa and Kanchan who also contributed to the photo shoot. I appreciate and thank my dedicated staff Gopinath, Mahadev, Naresh, Vijay, Dattu who are always willing to work and help. I thank everyone on the team of my publisher Popular Prakashan, who is associated with this book, for their help and co-operation. My close friends and my cooking class students don't go without being mentioned in my vote of thanks, as they are the ones eagerly waiting for my work. I thank them deeply for giving me the inspiration to write the recipes, cook them, perfect them and compiling them together in a book.

Contents

Author's Note

Gastronomy is never static and is evolving constantly, just like the visual arts and music. We too should be willing to re-evaluate the past in the light of current knowledge and consider new trends, with reference to dishes enjoyed by previous generations.

Nouvelle Indian Cuisine, the latest book in The Best of Epicure series, is a modern and experimental approach to traditional Indian cuisine.

This book also highlights the diversity of Indian food and its myriad different cooking techniques. It is about being unrestricted by old culinary notions and forging new ground, while using the best and most carefully chosen ingredients. This cuisine draws from rich Indian heritage not just in terms of ingredients, but technique as well. Indian food prepared with western sensibilities, modern styles of plating and serving, making it distinctively unique.

The concept of Nouvelle Indian cuisine was inspired by French nouvelle cuisine, began over a decade ago and is now on its way to becoming mainstream. The hallmarks of this cuisine are dishes plated aesthetically in a modern style that are also lighter on the palate.

To illustrate my point; young chefs today would enjoy interesting ways to blend, for example, gulab jamun into cheesecake mixture and pour it over a cracker crust base, creating a curry-flavoured risotto, converting spinach tempura into scrumptious chaat and so on.

As you open this book to enter the world of *Nouvelle Indian Cuisine* and discover the beautiful combination of the traditional and the modern, I am sure it will make cooking and eating an ever more pleasurable experience.

— **Asha Khatau**

Beverages

Coconut and Curry Leaves Soother

Ingredients

2 cups freshly grated coconut
12-15 fresh curry leaves
Black salt to taste
Lemon juice to taste

To garnish

Lemon slices and lemon grass stalks

To serve

Ice cubes

Method

Blend together the grated coconut, curry leaves and ½ cup water in a blender until smooth. Pass the mixture through a strainer, squeezing out all the juice. Add the black salt and a few drops of the lemon juice to taste.

Place 3-4 ice cubes in 2 glasses and pour the liquid over. Garnish with the lemon slices and provide lemon grass stalks as stirrers. Serve chilled.

Serves 2

Cucumber Buttermilk

Ingredients

3-4 medium cucumbers, peeled and sliced
Salt to taste
10-12 finely chopped mint leaves
2 cups yogurt
Black salt to taste
Cumin powder to taste

To garnish

Mint leaves

Method

Sprinkle the salt over the cucumbers and set aside for 30 minutes. Rinse and pat dry. Place the cucumbers, 2 cups ice-cold water with the remaining ingredients in a liquidiser jar and blend until mixed. Chill in the refrigerator. Serve in tall glasses and garnish with the mint leaves.

Serves 4-6

Fruit Salad Smoothie

Ingredients

1 cup chopped mixed fruit (banana, strawberries, apple, orange)

2 scoops vanilla ice cream

3-4 ice cubes

2 tbsp honey

Method

Place all the ingredients in a blender and blend until smooth. Pour into tall glasses and serve.

Serves 2

Ginger Rasam with Kaffir Lime Leaves

Ingredients

1 tbsp ghee or oil

8-10 black peppercorns

1½ tsp cumin seeds

1 dried red chilli, roasted

1 tbsp rasam powder

Salt to taste

2 tsp tamarind paste

1 tsp jaggery or ½ tsp sugar

2 large tomatoes, blanched and grated

½ tsp mustard seeds

2 pinches of asafoetida

2 garlic cloves, chopped

1-inch ginger, sliced

4 cups thin dal water

A few kaffir lime leaves

To garnish

Finely chopped coriander

Method

Heat ½ teaspoon ghee or oil and roast the peppercorns and 1 teaspoon cumin seeds until fragrant, then grind to a powder. Add the red chilli, rasam powder, salt, tamarind paste and jaggery. Blend all this with the grated tomatoes to a thick pulp. In a medium-sized pan, heat the remaining ghee; add the mustard seeds, remaining cumin seeds, asafoetida and allow it to splutter.

Add the garlic, ginger and stir in the tomato mixture. Add the thin dal water and check the seasoning. Add the kaffir lime leaves and simmer for 5-7 minutes. Garnish with the chopped coriander and serve hot in a glass.

Serves 6

Kala-Khatta Granita

Ingredients

¼ cup rock sugar
1-inch cinnamon stick
¼ cup lemon juice
2½ cups prepared kala-khatta

To garnish

6-8 black grapes rolled in powdered sugar, lemon slices

To serve

Salt-rimmed glasses

Method

Mix together the sugar, ¼ cup water and cinnamon in a pan and bring to a boil, stirring until the sugar dissolves. Remove from heat, add the lemon juice and cool slightly.

Purée the kala-khatta and sugar-lemon mixture in a blender. Transfer to a rectangular metal pan. Cover and freeze for several hours.

Using a fork, scrape the granita down the length of the pan, forming icy flakes. To serve, spoon scraped granita in each glass. Garnish with the sugared grapes, lemon slice and serve immediately.

Serves 6

Lemon Sherbet with Flavours

Ingredients

For the lemon sherbet

1 kg sugar

1 tbsp milk

1 cup fresh lemon juice

1 tsp citric acid

For the flavour options

1 tsp pure rose water or
1 tsp mint essence + a few mint leaves or
1 cup watermelon, cut into cubes or
1½ cups pineapple juice or
1½ cups orange juice or
1½ cups ginger ale

To garnish

Lemon slices, rose petals, orange slices, mint leaves, cubes of relevant fruits

To serve

Ice cubes

Method

In a heavy-bottomed pan, mix together the sugar and 1 litre water, place on medium heat and bring to a boil. When the sugar has melted add the milk and do not stir. The impurity of the sugar will float on top. Using a perforated spoon remove the scum and allow the mixture to attain a single-thread consistency.

Remove from heat and add the lemon juice and citric acid. Mix well. Add the preferred flavouring from the options provided. Cover and set aside overnight. Strain the syrup through a piece of muslin and fill in glass jars. Use as required.

For fresh fruit flavours, add the fruits, garnishes and ice cubes at the time of serving.

Makes 1 litre sherbet

Masala Iced Tea Punch

Ingredients

8 tsp black tea leaves
2 tsp Tea Masala (recipe follows)
¾ cup rock sugar, powdered
A handful of lemon grass
A handful of mint leaves
Juice of 2 lemons

To garnish

Lemon slices studded with cloves, slivered ginger, lemon grass stalks, cinnamon sticks, fresh mint leaves and whole cardamoms

To serve

Flavoured ice cubes

Method

Bring 4 cups water to a boil in a pan. Remove from heat and add the tea leaves, tea masala and sugar. Cover and set aside for 2-3 minutes. Remove the lid and add the lemon grass and mint leaves. Cool to room temperature.

Strain and add the lemon juice. Adjust the sugar to taste. Pour the mixture into a large punch bowl. Add all the garnishes to the bowl along with some ice cubes.

To serve, place 5-6 ice cubes at the bottom of each glass. Top with chilled tea and serve. Provide straws, which can be used as stirrers.

Serves 6

Tea Masala

Grind together 10 gm black peppercorns, 10 gm cinnamon, 10 gm cloves and 10 gm dried ginger and 40 gm whole cardamom to a smooth powder. Store in an airtight container.

Saffron-Almond/Jasmine/Rose Syrup Sherbet

Ingredients

For the basic syrup

1 kg sugar

1 tbsp milk

1 tbsp lemon juice

1 tsp citric acid

For the saffron-almond flavour

1 tsp powdered saffron

¼ cup slivered almonds

For the jasmine flavour

100 gm fresh jasmine flowers

For the rose flavour

50 gm dried rose petals or

100 gm fresh rose petals

Method

In a heavy bottomed-pan, mix together the sugar and 1 litre water, place on medium heat and bring to a boil. When the sugar has melted add the milk and do not stir. The impurity of the sugar will float on top. Using a perforated spoon remove the scum and allow the mixture to attain a single-thread consistency.

Remove from heat and add the lemon juice and citric acid. Mix well. Add the preferred flavouring from the options provided. Cover and set aside overnight. Strain the syrup through a piece of muslin and fill in glass jars. Use as required.

Makes 1 litre sherbet

Tip: For the jasmine and rose flavour, it is a good idea to wash and soak the flowers for 1 hour, in a little water taken from the 1 litre quota to get better flavour.

Left to Right – Beetroot and Aloo Tikki (page 28), Paneer Tikka Quesadillas (page 46), Curried Mushroom Bruschetta (page 34)

Clockwise – Channa Masala Hummus with Zatar Pav (page 32), Aloo Tokri Chaat (page 25), Black and White Sesame Paneer with Szechwan Cream (page 30)

Soups and Salads

Bhaji Minestrone

Ingredients

1 tbsp oil

1 medium onion, finely chopped

1 tbsp crushed garlic

1 medium green capsicum, finely chopped

1 tbsp red chilli paste

1-2 tsp pav-bhaji masala

Salt to taste

1 cup finely chopped vegetables (French beans, carrots, peas)

1 cup freshly puréed tomatoes

1 tbsp butter

Lemon to taste

To garnish
Finely chopped coriander and onions

To serve
Toasted and buttered ladi pav

Method

Heat the oil in a heavy-bottomed pan; add the onion, garlic and capsicum and sauté for 3-4 minutes. Add the red chilli paste, pav-bhaji masala, salt and cook for 3-4 minutes. Add the vegetables and cook until tender.

Add the puréed tomatoes and 1 cup water and simmer until all the ingredients are incorporated and the mixture begins to boil. Adjust the consistency by adding extra water. Add the butter and lemon juice as required.

Pour this into soup bowls, garnish with the chopped coriander, onion and serve with the ladi pav that has been cut into long pieces, toasted and buttered.

Serves 4

Chawli Salad

Ingredients

½ cup boiled corn kernels

½ cup finely diced carrots

½ cup celery

½ cup red capsicum

¾ cup dried black-eyed beans, soaked overnight and boiled

½ cup tomato

¼ cup finely chopped onion

2 tbsp lemon juice
1 tbsp freshly chopped herbs
¼ cup freshly chopped coriander
Salt to taste
Pepper to taste
Chaat masala to taste

Method

Place the corn, carrot, celery and capsicum into boiling hot water for 1 minute, then remove and drain. In a large bowl, combine the beans, corn, carrots, celery, capsicum, tomato, and onion. Add the lemon juice and toss well. Cover and place in the refrigerator for 30 minutes.

Thirty minutes before serving, add the chopped herbs, coriander, salt, pepper and chaat masala. Toss and serve.

Serves 8-10

Curried Sweetcorn Soup

Ingredients

1 cup corn kernels
½ cup grated sweetcorn or corn, from the cob
1 tsp sugar
1 tsp pepper
1 tsp curry powder
Salt to taste
5 tbsp cornflour mixed with 1 cup water

To garnish

Fried green chillies

Method

Boil the corn kernels in the pressure cooker with 6 cups water until the pressure is released 3 times (3 whistles). Remove once the pressure cooker is cool and place it in a wide pan.

Add the grated corn, sugar, pepper, curry powder and salt. Bring to a boil and simmer for 3 minutes. Add the cornflour mixture, stirring continuously, until the soup thickens. Bring to a boil and simmer for 1 minute, stirring continuously. Transfer to a soup bowl, garnish with the fried chillies and serve hot.

Serves 4

Mulligatawny Soup

Ingredients

1 tbsp butter
2 medium onions, chopped
2 garlic cloves, crushed
250 gm bottle gourd, cut into cubes
2 medium carrots, chopped
2 tomatoes, chopped
4 tbsp red lentils, washed and soaked
1 tsp curry powder
Salt to taste
Pepper to taste

To serve

Pieces of lemon, steamed rice

Method

Melt the butter in a pan and sauté the onions and garlic. Add all the vegetables, lentils and 4 cups water and cook in the pressure cooker until the pressure is released 4 times (4 whistles).

Let it cool and then process the soup in a blender, strain and return to heat. Add the curry powder, salt and pepper, and boil until thick. Serve hot with the lemon pieces and rice.

Serves 4

Smoked Papad Churi Salad

Ingredients

3-4 moong papads, roasted

¼ cup mashed potatoes

¼ cup thick yogurt

Salt to taste

Chaat masala to taste

Chilli powder to taste

Sugar to taste

1 cup iceberg lettuce leaves, torn into square pieces

½ cup spring onion, finely chopped

½ cup tomatoes

2 green chillies, seeded and chopped

1 piece burning charcoal in a small metal bowl

A few drops of oil

Method

Coarsely crush the papad into big pieces and place them in a wide pan or bowl. Move the papad pieces to the sides of the pan. Place the burning charcoal in a small metal bowl and place the bowl in the centre of the pan. Pour a few drops of oil over the charcoal and immediately cover the pan tightly with the lid. Keep covered until the coal stops smoking. Transfer the smoked papads to an airtight container.

Mix together the potatoes and yogurt in a small bowl. Add the salt, chaat masala, chilli powder and sugar. Set aside. Just before serving time, layer some of the papad churi, lettuce leaves, spring onion, tomato, green chillies and prepared potato cream in a transparent square or round glass jar. Repeat the layers twice. Cover the jar with the lid and serve immediately.

Serves 2

Water Chestnut and Peanut Salad

Ingredients

1½ cups peeled water chestnuts
1 cup boiled peanuts
½ tsp chaat masala
½ tsp sea salt
½ tsp chilli powder
½ tsp cumin powder
2-3 fresh red chillies, finely chopped
Juice of 1 lemon
Salt to taste
Sugar to taste

To garnish

Finely chopped coriander

To serve

Lettuce-lined plate

Method

Cut the water chestnuts in half and wash them in cold water. Drain and set aside. Place the boiled peanuts in a serving bowl; add the chaat masala, sea salt, chilli and cumin powders, chillies, lemon juice, salt and sugar. Add the water chestnuts and toss gently to mix.

Garnish with the chopped coriander and chill until ready to serve. Just before serving, transfer the salad to the lettuce-lined plate. Serve cold.

Serves 4

Snacks and Starters

Aloo ke Dahi Bhalle

Ingredients

6 medium potatoes, boiled and mashed
Salt to taste
1 tsp red chilli powder
2 tsp cumin powder
1 tsp garam masala
1 tsp chaat masala
3 tbsp finely chopped coriander
3-4 green chillies, chopped
6-8 white bread slices
2 cups yogurt
½ tsp black salt
Oil for shallow-frying

To garnish and serve

Chilli powder, cumin powder, chaat masala, finely chopped coriander, fresh pomegranate kernels, gram flour crispies

To serve

Sweet and Sour Chutney (page 97)

Method

Place the mashed potatoes in a wide bowl and add the salt, chilli powder, cumin powder, garam masala, chaat masala, 2 tablespoons chopped coriander, green chillies and mix well.

Cut the bread slices into 3-inch discs with a round cookie cutter. Apply a little water on the circular bread slices; just enough to let the potato mixture stick to the bread slices. Take approximately 2 tablespoons potato mixture and spread evenly on the bread, and smoothen the top. Heat the oil in a pan and fry the circular bread slices until golden brown. Drain on kitchen paper. Set aside to cool.

Beat the yogurt in a bowl, with the rock salt. When the circular bread slices are cool arrange them on a serving plate and pour the yogurt over. Garnish with the chilli powder, cumin powder, chaat masala, chopped coriander, pomegranate kernels, gram flour crispies and serve with the sweet and sour chutney.

Serves 6-8

Aloo Tokri Chaat

Ingredients

For the aloo tokri

250 gm potatoes (wafer variety), peeled and shredded

2-3 tbsp arrowroot flour

Salt to taste

Chilli powder to taste

Oil for frying

For the spice mix

4 (1-inch) cinnamon sticks

4 cardamoms

4 cloves

5-6 dried red chillies

5-6 sliced dried coconut

½ tsp sesame seeds

½ tsp cumin seeds

½ tsp coriander seeds

½ tsp aniseed

1 tsp pepper

1 tsp poppy seeds

1 tbsp oil

For the chaat

200 gm dried white or green peas, soaked overnight

1 tbsp oil

1 medium onion, finely chopped

1 medium tomato, finely chopped

½ tsp mustard seeds

½ tsp turmeric powder

½ tsp chilli powder

1 tbsp ginger-chilli paste

A few curry leaves

Salt to taste

1-2 tbsp tamarind pulp

1-2 tbsp jaggery

½ tsp dried mango powder

To garnish

Finely chopped coriander, shredded ginger

Method

For the aloo tokri, drain the shredded potatoes completely. Place them on a plate and add the arrowroot, salt and chilli powder.

Place 1-2 tablespoons potato mixture in a metal tea strainer and with the help of your thumb press in the mixture to take the circular shape of the strainer. Heat the oil on high heat. Dip the strainer in oil and remove it. Do this 2-3 times until the basket is golden in colour. Remove the basket carefully out of strainer and cool completely.

For the spice mix, roast the ingredients for the spice mix in 1 tablespoon oil until fragrant. Cool and powder the spices.

For the chaat, cook the peas in the pressure cooker until soft. Set aside. Heat 1 tablespoon oil in a pan and sauté onions until soft. Add the tomato and cook for 2 minutes. Add the mustard seeds, spice mix, turmeric powder, chilli powder, ginger-chilli paste and curry leaves. Fry for 3-4 minutes. Add the boiled peas along with the water they were boiled in, salt, tamarind pulp, jaggery and dried mango powder. Bring to a boil and simmer until the gravy is thick and all the liquid dries out. Remove from heat and set aside to cool.

To assemble chaat, place the aloo tokris on a serving platter, spoon 1-2 tablespoons peas mixture, garnish with the chopped coriander and ginger and serve immediately.

Serves 6-8

Amaranth Lavash with Yogurt Romesco Dip

Ingredients

For the lavash

¾ cup amaranth flour

¼ cup gram flour

1 tbsp olive oil

½ tsp salt

¼ cup black and white sesame seeds

For the Romesco dip

1 large red capsicum, grilled, peeled and chopped

¼ cup salted almonds, roughly chopped

1 tbsp apple cider vinegar

Salt to taste

Pepper to taste

1 cup thick yogurt

To garnish

Olive oil and chilli flakes

Method

For the lavash, mix together all the ingredients, except the sesame seeds, in a bowl and add water to bind and make a soft dough. Set aside for 10 minutes. Roll out the dough into a large square or rectangle. Halfway through rolling, sprinkle the sesame seeds and roll again so that the seeds get embedded in the dough. With a very sharp knife, cut into 7 x 2-inch triangle pieces. Preheated the oven at 160°C/320°F/Gas Mark 3 for 10 minutes. Arrange them on a baking tray and bake for 10-12 minutes. Remove and store in an airtight container.

For the Romesco dip, place the red capsicum, almonds, vinegar, salt and pepper in a small food processor. Process until smooth. Stir this mixture into the yogurt. Transfer to a serving bowl, garnish with the olive oil and chilli flakes. Serve with lavash.

Serves 6

Note: Originating from Spain, Romesco is a nut and red pepper based sauce.

Baigan Bharta in Savoury Cones

Ingredients

For the cone

1 cup sieved plain flour

½ tsp salt

1 tsp baking powder

¾ tsp soda bicarbonate

1 cup thick buttermilk

3 tbsp melted butter

For the bharta

2 large brinjals

3-4 tbsp oil + as required

1 tsp cumin seeds

3-4 garlic cloves, crushed

2 medium onions, finely chopped

3-4 medium tomatoes, blanched and chopped

Salt to taste

½ tsp sugar

1 tbsp garam masala

½ tsp turmeric powder

½ tsp chilli powder

To garnish

Finely chopped coriander

Method

For the cone, sieve the first four ingredients and place in a bowl. Add the buttermilk and butter and whisk so that there are no lumps left. Set aside for 30 minutes. Make a thin pancake on a hot griddle. While it is hot, carefully lift it up and place it in a cone-shaped mould. Allow it to set and take the shape of a cone. Remove when it is completely cooled and store in an air-tight container. Use as required. Makes 12-14 cones.

For the bharta, prick each brinjal with a fork and apply the oil over them using your palms. Roast each brinjal directly on the flame or on a barbecue grill until soft. Set aside to cool. Hold under running water and remove the skin. Place the brinjals on a plate and mash with a fork. Remove the stems. Set aside.

Heat the oil in a pan; sauté the cumin seeds, garlic and onion. Cook until soft. Add the tomatoes, salt, sugar and all the spices. Cook for 5-7 minutes. Add the mashed brinjals and mix well.

To assemble and serve, spoon 2-3 tablespoons bharta in each cone, garnish with the chopped coriander and serve immediately.

Serves 8-10

Note: To make potato bharta, use 500 gm potatoes and proceed in the same method as the brinjals. Instead of roasting the potatoes on the gas or grill, it is easier to bake them in the oven packed in foil.

Beetroot and Aloo Tikki

Ingredients

250 gm boiled beetroot
250 gm boiled potatoes
1 tbsp grated ginger
1 tbsp chopped green chillies
1 tbsp chopped garlic
¼ cup chopped coriander
¼ cup chopped mint
¼ cup breadcrumbs
2 tbsp toasted and chopped cashew nuts
Juice of 1 lemon
Salt to taste
Pepper to taste
Broken vermicelli to coat
Oil for shallow-frying

To garnish

Crisp potato sticks, shredded ginger and sprigs of mint

To serve

Mint raita

Method

Peel and grate the beetroot and potatoes. Add all the remaining ingredients, except the vermicelli and mix well. Roll the mixture into 2-inch round patties (tikki), roll each one in the vermicelli.

Heat the oil in a frying pan and fry the tikki in batches. Arrange 3 of them on a platter for individual serving; if serving all together place them on one side of the plate, overlapping. Garnish with the potato sticks, shredded ginger and place mint at the corner. Place a dollop of the mint raita on one side. Serve immediately.

Makes 8 tikki

Bengali-Style Mattar Kachori

Ingredients

For the dough

2 cups plain flour

2 tbsp ghee

1 tsp dried onion seeds

Salt to taste

For the peas stuffing

2 tsp oil

2 green chillies, finely chopped

½-inch ginger, chopped

1 tsp cumin powder

½ tsp chilli powder

½ tsp cardamom powder

½ tsp garam masala

A pinch of asafoetida

1 cup shelled peas, coarsely ground

Salt to taste

Sugar to taste

1 tbsp gram flour

Oil for deep-frying

To serve

Coriander-Mustard Sauce (recipe follows)

Method

For the dough, mix together all the ingredients in a bowl and add water little by little to make a soft dough. Cover with a cloth and set aside for 30 minutes.

For the peas stuffing, heat the oil in a frying pan and add the chilli, ginger, cumin powder, chilli powder, cardamom powder, garam masala and asafoetida. Fry for 5 seconds and add the ground peas, salt and sugar. Cook for 2-3 minutes. Mix well. Add the gram flour and cook further for 2-3 minutes and remove from heat. Transfer to a bowl and set aside to cool. Prepare small balls from the stuffing and set aside.

Heat the oil in a heavy-bottomed pan. Make lemon-sized ball of the dough, and roll into 3-inch diameter circles. Place the stuffing in the centre and bring all the edges of the dough together and press them together. Grease your palms with a little oil if required. Roll out 4-5-inch circles and gently slide it into the hot oil. With a slotted spoon, apply gentle pressure on the kachori to help it puff up. Once one side is puffed up, turn over and fry for a few seconds until it turns golden in colour. Drain on kitchen paper. Serve hot with the coriander-mustard sauce.

Makes 8-10 kachori

Coriander-Mustard Sauce

Blend together ¼ cup kashundi mustard sauce with ½ cup chopped coriander, 1-2 green chillies, salt and sugar to taste. Add chilled water to achieve the required consistency.

Makes ¾ cup

Black and White Sesame Paneer with Szechwan Cream

Ingredients

400 gm soft cottage cheese, cut into 1-inch cubes

2 tbsp sesame oil

1 tsp salt

1 tsp pepper

1 tsp crushed garlic

5 tbsp black and white sesame seeds, toasted

¼ cup thick Szechwan sauce

¼ cup mayonnaise

½ cup whipped cream

To garnish

Crisp rice noodles and sprigs of coriander

To serve

A set of rounded soup spoons

Method

Soak the cottage cheese pieces in chilled mineral water for 20-30 minutes. Drain and place on a plate. Drizzle the sesame oil over and then sprinkle each piece with the salt, pepper, and crushed garlic.

Place the sesame seeds in a small plate. Coat each cottage cheese piece with the sesame seeds and arrange on a greased baking tray. Bake in a pre-heated oven at 180°C/350°F/Gas Mark 4 for 5-7 minutes. Keep warm.

Blend together the Szechwan sauce and mayonnaise until smooth and creamy. Fill this mixture into a syringe with a star nozzle. Transfer the cottage cheese pieces to a small bowl and fold in the whipped cream.

Arrange the spoon on a serving tray. Place the crisp noodles at the bottom and place each piece over the noodles. Pipe stars of the prepared cream on each one.

Garnish with the coriander sprigs and serve at once.

Makes 16 pieces

Chaat in a Jar

Ingredients

1 tbsp oil
½ tsp cumin seeds
A few curry leaves
1-2 green chillies, slit
250 gm sprouts of your choice
250 gm shelled green peas
Black salt to taste
Salt to taste
1 tbsp dried mango powder
1 medium potato, boiled and finely chopped
1 medium tomato, finely chopped
1 medium onion, finely chopped
1 tbsp finely chopped coriander
1 tbsp finely chopped green chillies
Lemon juice to taste
¼ cup Green Chutney (page 93)
¼ cup Date and Tamarind Chutney (page 93)
100 gm spinach sev or any gram flour crispies

To serve

Masala buttermilk (i.e. buttermilk mixed with jiralu and coriander)

Method

Heat the oil in a pan, fry the cumin seeds, curry leaves and chillies. Add the sprouts and peas. Sprinkle a little water to avoid sticking.

Cook uncovered until soft. Add the black salt, salt and dried mango powder. Mix well. Mix the potato, tomato, onion, coriander, chopped green chillies and lemon juice in a small bowl.

Take 4 small transparent jars and layer half of sprout mixture and alternating with the tomato mixture, sweet and green chutney in each one.

Top it with the spinach sev or gram flour crispies. Serve with the masala buttermilk.

Serves 4

Channa Masala Hummus with Zatar Pav

Ingredients

For the channa masala hummus

250 gm chickpeas, soaked for 6 hours
½ tsp turmeric powder
½ tsp salt
2 big cardamoms, peeled
3-4 tbsp oil
2 medium onions, chopped
4 small green chillies, slit
1-inch ginger, thinly sliced
3-4 garlic cloves, chopped (optional)
2 tbsp chilli powder
2 tbsp coriander-cumin powder
1 tbsp garam masala
1 tbsp dried mango powder
1 tbsp pepper
1 tbsp garam masala
1 tsp black salt
1 tsp big cardamom seeds
½ cup tomato purée
Salt to taste

For the zatar pav

2 tbsp butter
6-8 ladi pav
2 tbsp zatar spice mix

To garnish

Sliced onions and finely chopped coriander

Method

For the channa masala hummus, cook the chickpeas in the pressure cooker with turmeric powder, salt and cardamom seeds. Heat the oil in a pan and fry the onions, green chillies, ginger and garlic (if using) until soft.

Add all the dry spices along with the boiled chickpeas, tomato pureé and salt. Cook until the mixture is thick. Remove from heat and cool completely. Place the prepared chickpeas in a blender to make a smooth paste. Transfer to a serving bowl and garnish with the onion and chopped coriander.

For the zatar pav, cut the pav into halves. Heat the butter in a small frying pan and toast the pav until golden. Garnish with the zatar spice mix and serve with the prepared hummus.

Serves 6-8

Cheese Papad Rolls

Ingredients

4 thin moong papads

250 gm processed cheese, cut into 1-inch sticks

Oil for deep-frying

To garnish

1 tsp chilli powder

Method

Place the papads on a flat surface and moisten with just enough water to soften them. Cut each one into 1-inch strips. Place a cheese stick at the edge of each papad strip and roll it up lightly. Secure the ends with a toothpick.

Holding one end of the toothpick, deep-fry the roll in hot oil. Remove and drain on kitchen paper. Garnish with the chilli powder and serve hot.

Serves 6

Chilli Paneer Wraps

Ingredients

For the wrappers

1 tsp plain flour

1 tsp cornflour

½ tsp salt

For the filling

200 gm cottage cheese, cut into ½-inch cubes

1 tbsp butter

1 tbsp oil

4-5 green chillies, slit length-wise

1 tbsp crushed ginger

1 tbsp crushed garlic

1 tbsp red chilli paste

½ tsp salt

½ tsp pepper

½ tsp sugar

1 tbsp soy sauce

1 tbsp chilli sauce

½ tbsp vinegar

2 spring onion stems, cut long

1 tbsp finely chopped coriander

10-12 iceberg lettuce leaves

To garnish

Crisp rice sticks and crushed peanuts

To serve

Toothpicks

Method

For the wrappers, mix together in a bowl the plain flour, cornflour and salt.

For the filling, roll the cottage cheese cubes in the flour mixture. Set aside. Heat the butter and oil together in a frying pan and fry the green chillies, ginger, garlic and chilli paste. Add the salt, pepper, sugar, soy sauce, chilli sauce, vinegar and mix well. Add a little water to avoid sticking. Add the cottage cheese cubes, spring onion stems and coriander and mix well.

Take a piece of the iceberg lettuce, place 2 tablespoons warm cottage cheese mixture, garnish with the rice sticks and peanuts. Wrap the lettuce to make a roll and insert a toothpick to hold and serve.

Serves 4

Curried Mushroom Bruschetta

Ingredients

3-4 tbsp oil
1 large onion, grated
3-4 garlic cloves, crushed
2 tsp pav-bhaji masala
1 tsp chilli powder (optional)
250 fresh mushrooms, stemmed, washed and halved
2 medium tomatoes, grated
Salt to taste
10-12 slices toasted baguette
Grated cheese to sprinkle
2 tbsp coriander leaves, finely chopped

Method

Heat the oil in a frying pan, fry the onion and garlic till soft. Make sure it does not stick. Add the pav-bhaji masala and chilli powder and fry for 2-3 minutes. When the oil starts separating add the mushrooms. Cook until the mushrooms are soft but firm. Add the tomatoes and salt. Cook further until all the liquid dries out.

Take 1 slice of the toasted baguette, and spread 1-2 tbsp mixture evenly. Sprinkle with the grated cheese and place under the hot grill for 3-4 minutes. Sprinkle with the chopped coriander. Serve hot.

Serves 4

Curry Fondue

Ingredients

1 tbsp sesame oil
2-3 garlic cloves, crushed
¼ cup finely chopped capsicum
1 tbsp curry powder
1 tbsp red chilli paste
½ cup diced vegetables of your choice
Salt to taste
1 cup vegetable stock
1 tbsp corn flour
1 cup grated fondue cheese
¼ cup finely chopped spring onions
Sugar to taste

To serve

Toasted bread, rice crackers or grilled vegetable pieces

Method

Heat the oil in a fondue dish on a low heat and sauté the garlic and capsicum for 1 minute. Add the curry powder, red chilli paste, diced vegetables and salt to taste. Cook for 2-3 minutes. Sprinkle a little water if required.

Add the vegetable stock and bring the mixture to a boil. Toss the corn flour into the cheese and gradually add spoonful to the boiling stock, stirring continuously. Simmer until the mixture is thick and creamy. Finally add the spring onion, salt and sugar to taste. Serve simmering hot fondue with the toasted bread, rice crackers or grilled vegetables.

Serves 4

Dabeli Tacos

Ingredients

For the dabeli

Oil, as required + for deep-frying

2 tbsp dabeli masala

2 medium tomatoes, grated

3-4 medium potatoes, boiled, peeled, and mashed

Salt to taste

For the masala peanuts

1 tsp oil

1 tbsp dabeli masala

⅓ cup peanuts, roasted and peeled

For the tacos

8 ladi pav, halved

Garlic chutney, as required

Sweet and Sour Chutney (page 97), as required (optional)

Butter, as required

To garnish

Finely chopped coriander and onions

Method

For the dabeli, heat the oil in a frying pan, sauté the dabeli masala, add the grated tomato, when cooked add the mashed potato. Cook for 5 minutes and add the salt.

For the masala peanuts, heat the oil in a frying pan and roast the dabeli masala and peanuts. Cook for 2 minutes and remove from heat and set aside.

For the tacos, place all the pav on a tray and apply the garlic chutney and sweet and sour chutney (if using) as per one's taste. Take the base of the pav and roll over it with a rolling pin to flatten it slightly. Spread the butter over the pav and gently fold it to form a crescent. Secure the shape with the help of a toothpick. Repeat for the remaining pav. Place all of them on an oven tray and bake until crisp.

To serve, fill each taco shell with ¼ cup potato mixture, garnish with the chopped coriander, masala peanuts and onions. Serve immediately.

Makes 16 tacos

Dosa Waffles

Ingredients

2 cups ready-made dosa batter

Salt to taste

1 tsp fruit salt

Butter for greasing

To garnish

Mulgapodi powder

To serve

Tomato Chutney (page 98), and banana leaf

Method

Remove the dosa batter from the packet and make sure it is at room temperature. At the time of making waffles, add the salt and fruit salt with ¼ cup warm water and add to the batter.

Heat the waffle iron, brush it with butter and pour approximately ½ cup batter; making sure it covers all the corners of the waffle plate. Shut the lid and cook the waffle until golden in colour.

Transfer to a plate lined with the banana leaf and garnish with the mulgapodi powder. Serve hot with the tomato chutney.

Makes 8 waffles

Edamame Samosa

Ingredients

250 gm plain flour

1 tbsp oil

For the filling

1 tbsp sesame oil

3-4 green chillies, coarsely chopped

500 gm fresh or frozen edamame, coarsely ground

Salt to taste

Juice of 1 lemon

2 tbsp finely chopped coriander

Oil for deep-frying

To serve

Finely chopped coriander

Coriander-Peanut Pesto (recipe follows)

Method

Combine the plain flour, oil and water to make a semi-soft dough. Cover and set aside. Heat the sesame oil in a frying pan and fry the chillies for 2 minutes.

Add a little water if the mixture sticks to the pan. Cook for 3-4 minutes. Add the edamame, salt and a little more water. Cook until tender and the mixture is dry. Add the lemon juice and chopped coriander. Set aside to cool.

Divide the dough into 8 portions. Place a portion in the middle of your palm and shape it into a disc. Now place this on a board and roll it with a rolling pin to 4-5-inch diameter disc. Cut this into half. Fold each half to form a cone shape, stick ends with some water.

Stuff 1 tablespoon edamame mixture and seal the edges using little water. Repeat for the rest of the portions. Fry them in hot oil until crisp. Serve hot with the chopped coriander and peanut pesto.

Makes 8 samose

Coriander-Peanut Pesto

Place 2 cups coarsely chopped coriander leaves, ¼ cup skinless peanuts, 7-8 green chillies; 1-inch chopped ginger, 1 tablespoon sugar; 1 tablespoon oil; 1 teaspoon cumin seeds; juice of 1 lemon; salt to taste; in a grinder and make a paste. Use a little water if necessary. Store in refrigerator.

Makes 1 cup

Kokum Saar Sorbet

Ingredients

1 cup thick coconut milk
2 tbsp kokum juice
1 tsp salt
1 tsp sugar
A pinch of asafoetida
A few curry leaves
2-3 garlic cloves, chopped
2-3 green chillies, chopped

For the tempering

1 tbsp oil
1 tsp cumin seeds

Method

Blend together the coconut milk with kokum juice, salt and sugar. Transfer this mixture to a container and place in the freezer for 6 hours or overnight. Remove the mixture from the freezer and blend in a blender once again and return to the freezer for another 4-5 hours or until frozen.

For the tempering, heat the oil in a small pan and add the cumin seeds. When they splutter add the asafoetida, curry leaves, garlic, chillies and 1 tablespoon water. To serve the sorbet, remove 1 scoop and place in a bowl. Sprinkle 1 teaspoon tempering over each scoop and serve.

Serves 6-8

Lentil Waffles

Ingredients

⅓ cup skinless split black gram
⅓ cup split Bengal gram
⅓ cup skinless split green gram
1 tomato, finely chopped
1 onion, finely chopped
3-4 green chillies, finely chopped
¼ cup finely chopped coriander
¼ tsp turmeric powder
1 tbsp oil + for greasing
A pinch of asafoetida
Salt to taste

To serve

Coconut Chutney (page 92)

Method

Soak all the grams together for 3-4 hours and grind them with some water to make a coarse batter of dropping consistency. Mix together all the other ingredients with the batter and set aside for 1 hour.

Heat a waffle iron and brush it with a little oil. When the iron is very hot, pour enough mixture to cover all the corners of the iron and lightly close the lid. Cook till the waffles are golden brown. Serve hot with the coconut chutney.

Makes 6-8 waffles

Makai ke Dahi Bhalle

Ingredients

¾ cup skinless split black gram, soaked for 6 hours

½ cup crushed fresh corn

1 tbsp ginger-chilli paste

2 tbsp gram flour

1 tbsp curry powder

Salt to taste

Oil for frying

To garnish

1 cup thick yogurt

Salt to taste

Sugar to taste

¼ cup Sweet and Sour Chutney (page 97)

¼ cup Green Chutney (page 93)

1 tsp roasted cumin powder

1 tsp chilli powder

1 tsp chaat masala

½ cup crisp boondi

Finely chopped coriander

Method

Grind the split black gram with a little water, to make a smooth paste. Transfer to a bowl and add the corn, ginger-chilli paste, gram flour, curry powder and salt.

Beat the paste well with your palm for 5-7 minutes, or until the mixture looks fluffy. Heat the oil in a deep pan and drop 1 tablespoon mixture, 6-7 dumplings at a time. Fry on medium heat until golden. Drain on kitchen paper. Repeat for the remaining batter.

Drop the cooled dumplings into a bowl with 2-3 cups water. Soak until they are almost double in size and soft. Remove and squeeze out the water completely. Arrange them on a serving platter. Mix together the yogurt, salt, sugar and churn. Pour this over the prepared dumplings, followed by the sweet and sour chutney, and green chutney. Garnish with the powdered spices, boondi and chopped coriander. Place in the refrigerator until ready to serve.

Serves 4-6

Makai Malai Methi Kababs

Ingredients

1 cup crushed or grated American corn
1 cup grated cottage cheese
½ boiled and grated potato
½ cup corn kernels, boiled
2-3 tbsp fresh cream
2 tbsp ginger-chilli-garlic paste
Salt to taste
1 tbsp dried fenugreek leaves
Cornflour to bind
Oil for frying

To garnish

Chopped coriander

To serve

Coriander-Mustard Sauce (page 29)

Method

In a medium-sized bowl, place the grated corn, cottage cheese, grated potato, corn kernels, fresh cream, ginger-chilli-garlic paste, salt and mix well. Crush the dried fenugreek leaves with your fingers and add along with the cornflour, 1 tablespoon at a time. Mix with your palm until the mixture does not stick. Make either circular or cylindrical shaped kababs and roll in the cornflour to get a smooth finish.

Heat the oil in a heavy-bottomed frying pan, shallow-fry the kababs in batches until golden in colour. Drain on kitchen paper. Garnish with the chopped coriander and serve hot with the coriander-mustard sauce.

Makes 6-8 kababs

Makai Vada in Misal Rasa

Ingredients

For the vada

¾ cup grated fresh corn
2 tbsp maize flour
1 tbsp ginger-chilli paste
1 tbsp gram flour
½ cup finely chopped spring onions
½ tsp soda bicarbonate
Salt to taste
Oil for deep-frying

For the spice mix

2 tbsp oil
2 tbsp coriander seeds
1 tbsp sesame seeds
2-inch cinnamon stick
3-4 cloves
5-6 peppercorns
8-10 dried red chillies, broken
1 tbsp Kashmiri red chilli powder (optional)
1 small piece dried coconut, sliced

For the rasa

½ cup fresh tomato purée
2 tbsp spice mix paste (spice mix + water)
2 tbsp ginger-garlic paste
½ cup boiled corn or sprouts
2 tbsp jaggery and tamarind paste
Salt to taste

For the top tempering

2 tbsp oil
2 tbsp spice mix paste (spice mix + water)
A few curry leaves

To garnish

Finely chopped coriander, grated coconut

To serve

Fried crisps and lemon wedges

Method

For the vada, mix together all the ingredients in a bowl and make a stiff mixture. Shape into walnut-sized balls and gently press to make a patties. Set aside. Deep-fry in hot oil, in batches at the time of serving.

For the spice mix, heat the oil in a small frying pan and roast all the spices except the chilli powder, and dried coconut, until fragrant. Remove from heat and allow it to cool. Add the red chilli powder (if using). Grind in a dry grinder and fill in a jar. Use as required.

For the rasa, mix together all the ingredients along with 1-2 cups water, in a pan and bring to a gentle boil.

For the top tempering, heat the oil in a small pan and add the spice mix paste and curry leaves. Fry for 1-2 minutes. Pour this over the boiling liquid gravy (rasa).

To serve, take individual soup bowls; place 2-3 hot corn vada at the bottom. Pour over the hot boiling rasa until the bowl is three-quarters full. Garnish with the chopped coriander and grated coconut and serve with the fried crisps and lemon wedges on the side.

Serves 4-6

Masala Puri Chaat with Trio of Peas

Ingredients

For the puri

½ cup white gram flour
¼ cup plain flour
1½ cups semolina
2 tbsp whole-wheat flour
1 tbsp oil
Salt to taste
Oil for frying

For the peas mixture

1 tbsp oil
½ tsp cumin seeds
3-4 green chillies, slit lengthwise
1-inch ginger, grated
¼ tsp asafoetida
2 medium onions, finely chopped
½ tsp cumin powder
½ tsp garam masala
1 tsp red chilli powder
¼ tsp turmeric powder
Salt to taste
100 gm dried black peas, soaked and boiled
100 gm dried green peas, soaked and boiled
100 gm dried white peas, soaked and boiled
1 tbsp tamarind paste

To assemble

2 medium potatoes, boiled, peeled and mashed
Finely chopped onion, as required
Finely chopped tomatoes, as required
½ cup Green Chutney (page 93)
½ cup Date and Tamarind Chutney (page 93)
½ cup thick yogurt

To garnish

Finely chopped coriander, sev and a few fresh pomegranate kernels

Method

For the puri, combine all the ingredients, adding water slowly and make a dough. Cover and set aside for 30 minutes. Knead the dough again and divide it into very small balls. Roll them out into small thin puri using a 2-inch round cutter.

Heat the oil in a deep pan, once hot reduce to medium heat, slide the puri 3-4 at a time, frying on both sides. Store in a container and use as required. Makes 18-20 puri.

For the peas mixture, heat the oil in a shallow pan, add the cumin seeds. When they splutter, add the green chillies, ginger and sauté for 10-15 seconds. Add the asafoetida, followed by the onions. Cook until soft.

Add the powdered spices and salt. Add the boiled peas along with some water from the peas. Lightly mash the peas and cook for 5-7 minutes. Add the tamarind paste and cook for 2-3 minutes. The gravy should be thick. Remove from heat and garnish with the chopped tomatoes and chopped coriander.

To assemble the chaat, take a wide serving plate, roughly crush some of the puri and layer at the bottom of the plate. Next, layer it with the mashed potatoes and top it with the warm peas mixture, onion, tomatoes, green chutney and date and tamarind chutney. Gently spoon the thick yogurt over and the sev. Finally garnish with the chopped coriander and fresh pomegranate kernels. Serve immediately.

Serves 8

Paneer and Jalapeño Balls

Ingredients

1 cup crumbled cottage cheese

1 cup shredded Cheddar cheese

½ cup diced jalapeño chillies

¼ cup plain flour

Salt to taste

Breadcrumbs to roll

Oil for deep-frying

To serve

Sour Cream (page 96) and
Red Salsa (page 96)

Method

Combine both the cheeses, jalapeño chillies, flour and salt in a medium-sized bowl. Mix well to form a soft dough. Shape like thick chillies or cone shapes. Add a little milk if you find the mixture a little dry.

Roll each one in the breadcrumbs and deep-fry in hot oil. Serve with the sour cream and salsa.

Makes 16 servings

Paneer Tikka Quesadillas

Ingredients

250 gm cottage cheese, cubed
1 capsicum, seeded and cubed
1 onion, seeded and cubed
1 tomato, seeded and cubed
3 tbsp oil
2-3 tbsp tandoori masala paste
1 tbsp red chilli paste
1 medium onion, grated
¼ cup tomato purée
Salt to taste
½ cup yogurt, beaten
8 (5-inch) flour tortillas

To serve

Tomato-Mint Salsa (recipe follows) and sliced onions

Method

Mix together the cottage cheese and vegetables in a wide bowl. Heat 2 tablespoons oil in a frying pan and add the tandoori paste, chilli paste and grated onion. Fry for 3-4 minutes. Add the tomato purée, salt and yogurt. Mix well.

Remove from heat and pour over the cottage cheese and vegetables. Cover and set aside for 45 minutes or more. Grease a frying pan or a baking dish with 1 tablespoon oil. Either sauté the cottage cheese and vegetables or place under a grill until golden brown. Remove from heat and set aside to cool. Mash the mixture with a fork. Place the tortilla on a work surface; spread 2-3 tablespoons cottage cheese mixture, flattening it out nicely. Cover with another tortilla and stick the edges.

Heat a frying pan and cook this tortilla sandwich on both sides until slightly crisp. Remove from the pan, cut into 4 triangles and serve with the tomato-mint salsa and sliced onions.

Serves 4

Tomato-Mint Salsa

Blend together 3-4 garlic cloves, 1 chopped onion, 2 tablespoons chopped jalapeños, 1 tablespoon chopped coriander, 1 tablespoon chopped mint, 1 tablespoon vinegar, 1 teaspoon taco seasoning, a pinch of oregano, 2 cups chopped red tomatoes, and salt to taste. Refrigerate until use.

Makes 1½ cups

Paneer, Cheese and Corn Bhajia

Ingredients

1½ cups grated cottage cheese
1 cup boiled corn
½ cup grated Cheddar cheese
1 tbsp finely chopped coriander
1 tsp chaat masala
1 tbsp finely chopped green chillies
1 tbsp green chilli-ginger-garlic paste
Salt to taste
3 tbsp cornflour
Oil for deep-frying

To serve

Ketchup or Green Chutney (page 93)

Method

Combine the cottage cheese, corn, cheese, coriander, chaat masala, chopped green chillies, chilli-ginger-garlic paste, salt and cornflour in a bowl and bind together. Place this mixture in the refrigerator for 30 minutes and remove.

Heat the oil in a kadai. Place a tablespoon of the mixture in hot oil and fry the dumplings in batches. Drain on kitchen paper. Serve hot with the ketchup or green chutney.

Serves 12

Left to Right – Dosa Waffles (page 37), Panipuri Crêpes (page 77)

Table Top Mixed Chaat (page 83)

To garnish

Sweet mango chutney, oil from a pickle, chopped coriander and shredded lettuce

Method

For the mango salsa, combine all the ingredients together in a bowl and mix well. Set aside.

For the spiced yogurt, mix together all the ingredients except boondi, in a bowl and chill. Add the boondi just before serving.

To assemble at the time of serving, place the roasted papad on a plate, spoon mango salsa onto each papad and top it with spiced yogurt. Garnish with the sweet mango chutney, oil from a pickle, chopped coriander and shredded lettuce. Serve immediately.

Serves 8

Root Vegetable Kabab Chaat

Ingredients

250 gm potato
250 gm sweet potato
250 gm pink yam
250 gm yellow yam
Oil for cooking
Chaat masala to taste
Chilli powder to taste
Roasted cumin powder to taste
Pepper to taste
Black salt to taste
Salt to taste
Lemon juice to taste
A few barbecue sticks, soaked in water

To garnish

Chopped coriander and yogurt

Method

Boil all the vegetables in the pressure cooker until the pressure is released 3 times (3 whistles). Remove from the cooker and cool completely. Cut each one into small cubes. Take a barbecue stick and thread 1 piece of each vegetable on it. Repeat this for the remaining vegetable.

Heat the oil in a flat frying pan, place 3-4 threaded sticks on it and cook on medium heat, turning the sides. Cook until all sides are brown. In a small bowl mix together the chaat masala, chilli powder, cumin powder, pepper, black salt and salt. Remove the barbecue stick from the pan and sprinkle with the spice mix and lemon juice. Garnish with the coriander and yogurt. Serve at once.

Serves 8

Spinach Tempura Chaat

Ingredients

For the spinach tempura

10-12 large spinach leaves, trimmed and washed

½ cup tempura batter mix

Oil for frying

For the chaat

½ cup finely chopped onion

½ cup finely chopped tomato

½ cup finely chopped boiled potato

¼ cup finely chopped unripe mango

¼ cup boiled chickpeas

¼ cup coriander leaves

¼ cup sev

¼ cup boondi

2 tbsp Sweet and Sour Chutney (page 97)

2 tbsp Green Chutney (page 93)

½ tsp chaat masala

½ tsp chilli powder

½ tsp salt

To garnish

Gram flour sev and chopped coriander

Method

For the spinach tempura, dry the spinach leaves thoroughly. Mix the tempura batter mix with ½ cup chilled water at the time of frying. Heat the oil in a pan; dip each leaf into the batter and fry in batches. Drain on kitchen paper and set aside.

For the chaat, in a medium-sized bowl, mix together all the ingredients for the chaat and toss gently to mix. Place prepared spinach leaves on a serving platter and put 2-3 tablespoons of this mixture over each leaf. Garnish with the sev and chopped coriander and serve at once.

Serves 6

Sprouted Green Moong Rissole Chaat

Ingredients

¼ kg sprouted whole green gram

3 green chillies, chopped

2 garlic cloves, crushed (optional)

3 tbsp chopped coriander

Salt to taste

1 tsp toasted sesame seeds

1 medium onion, finely chopped

Oil for deep-frying

To garnish

Thick yogurt, Green Chutney (page 93), garlic chutney, coriander leaves and fried chillies

Method

Grind together the sprouted green gram, chillies, garlic (if using) and chopped coriander, to make a thick paste. Add the salt and sesame seeds. Just before frying the rissoles add the onion. Mix well before frying. Place two tablespoons mixture onto the palm of your hand and shape into small balls.

Drop the balls into the hot oil and fry 8-10 at a time on medium heat. Drain on kitchen paper. On a serving plate, arrange them one on top of the other like a tower and drizzle the yogurt, green chutney and garlic chutney. Garnish with the coriander leaves and scatter fried chillies around. Serve at once.

Makes approximately 24 rissoles

Stir-Fried Vegetables Stuffed Dosa

Ingredients

For the stir-fried vegetables

100 gm baby corn

100 gm broccoli

100 gm bean sprouts

100 gm capsicums

2 tbsp oil

1 tsp finely chopped garlic

¼ cup vegetable stock mixed with 1 tsp cornflour

1 tbsp soy sauce

½ tsp salt

½ tsp pepper

½ tsp sugar

For the dosa

2 cups ready-made dosa batter

Oil for cooking

To serve

Chilli sauce

Method

For the stir fried vegetables, cut all the vegetables into 2-inch pieces at a slant.

Heat the oil in a wok, fry the garlic briefly and add the vegetables. Stir-fry for 2-3 minutes. Add the vegetable stock, soy sauce, salt, pepper and sugar. Do not over-cook the vegetables. Set aside.

For the dosa, heat the dosa pan and brush with a little oil. Spread ½ cup dosa batter at a time, to form a thin crêpes. Allow it to cook for 2-3 minutes and spread ¼ cup stir-fried vegetables in the centre. Fold over from both sides. Serve at once with the chilli sauce.

Serves 4-6

Stuffed Chilli Tempura

Ingredients

½ cup coriander leaves, finely chopped
½ cup coconut, grated
3-4 tbsp peanuts, roasted and powdered
1 tsp sugar
Salt to taste
Juice of ½ a lemon
1 tbsp ginger-chilli paste
2 medium potatoes, boiled and mashed
2 tbsp oil
1 tsp cumin seeds
½ kg Bhavnagri chillies, slit vertically
½ cup tempura batter mix
Oil for frying

To serve

Sweet and Sour Chutney (page 97)

Method

Mix together the chopped coriander, coconut, peanuts, sugar, salt, lemon juice and ginger-chilli paste. Toss lightly to mix, add the potatoes and salt, set aside. Heat 2 tablespoons oil in a small pan and add the cumin seeds. When they splutter add to the potato mixture. Mix well.

Stuff the slit chillies with this mixture. Mix the tempura batter mix with ½ cup chilled water. Dip the stuffed chillies in this batter and fry in hot oil immediately. Fry 4-5 pieces at a time. Serve hot with the sweet and sour chutney.

Serves 6

Thepla Quesadillas

Ingredients

For the thepla

1 cup whole-wheat flour

¼ cup gram flour

1 tsp chilli powder

1 tsp ginger-chilli paste

1 tsp coriander-cumin powder

¼ tsp turmeric powder

1 medium onion, grated

2 tbsp oil

Salt to taste

Sour yogurt to bind the dough

Oil for shallow-frying

For the filling

2 tbsp oil

1 tsp mustard seeds

1 tsp sesame seeds

A few curry leaves

2 cups green peas, boiled and crushed

2 tbsp green chilli-ginger paste

Salt to taste

Sugar to taste

Juice of 1 lemon

4 tbsp grated coconut

4 tbsp chopped coriander

¼ cup beaten rice, soaked in water

To serve

Sweet mango pickle

Method

For the thepla, mix both the flours along with all the dry spices, onion, 2 tbsp oil and salt. Bind into a semi-soft dough by adding the yogurt. Do not add water. Divide the dough into 12-14 balls. Roll out each one into a flat, thin 4-inch discs. Cook the theplas over medium heat, using a little oil. Cook each thepla on both sides on a hot tawa, drizzling with a little oil around the edges.

For the filling, heat the oil in a small pan, add the mustard and sesame seeds, when they begin to splutter, add curry leaves and peas. Cook for 3-4 minutes. Add the chilli-ginger paste, salt, sugar and lemon juice. Mix well. Remove from heat and add the coconut, coriander and soaked beaten rice. Mix well and set aside to cool completely.

To assemble, place 1 thepla on the cutting board, spoon ¼ cup filling in the centre and spread evenly. Slightly wet the edge of the thepla and stick another thepla to seal, just like a quesadilla. Place the thepla on a dry griddle and heat on both sides for a minute. Remove and cut into 4 pieces. Serve with the sweet mango pickle.

Makes 6 quesadillas

White Dhokla Roll-Ups

Ingredients

2 tbsp oil + for greasing
2 cups ready-made dhokla/idli batter
1 tbsp lemon juice
2 tsp fruit salt
1 tbsp ginger-chilli paste
Red chilli powder to taste
Pepper to taste
1 recipe Peanut Pesto (recipe follows)

To garnish

Sukha sambhar mixed with little oil

Method

For the dhokla, make sure that a large vessel filled with water is kept on heat boiling. Place a 5-inch circular ring at the bottom of the vessel. Grease 2 (9-inch) round stainless steel plates with rims, with the oil. Place 1 plate on the ring over boiling water. Make 1 plate of dhokla at a time.

Place 1 cup of the batter in a small bowl. In another small bowl mix together 2 tablespoons warm water, 1 teaspoon each of the lemon juice, oil and fruit salt. Add this to the batter along with ½ tbsp ginger-chilli paste and mix well.

Pour into the steel plate which is on boiling water. Sprinkle chilli powder on half and pepper powder on the other half. Cover with a lid. Cook for 7-10 minutes. Remove and transfer the set dhokla onto a cutting board. Repeat the same process for the second plate.

Spread the peanut pesto evenly over the dhokla and then roll in a jelly-roll fashion. Cut it at an angle into 2-inch pieces. Arrange on a serving platter slightly overlapping each other. Garnish with the sukha sambhar and serve warm.

Makes 20-22 roll-ups

Peanut Pesto

Place 2 cups finely chopped coriander leaves, ¼ cup grated coconut, ¼ cup roasted peanuts, 3-4 green chillies, 1-inch ginger, 1 teaspoon sugar, juice of ½ a lemon, 2 tablespoons olive oil, and salt to taste, in a small grinder and make a coarse paste. Use as required.

Makes 1 cup

Main Course

Aachari Aloo Paratha Pizza

Ingredients

For the paratha

400 gm potatoes, boiled and cut into cubes
2 tbsp mango pickle masala
1 cup whole-wheat flour
1 tbsp oil
Salt to taste
Oil for cooking

For the topping

1 tbsp oil
1 cup finely chopped onions
1 cup finely chopped capsicum
2 medium tomatoes, finely chopped
Salt to taste
1 tsp pizza seasoning
150 gm pizza cheese

To serve

Thick yogurt

Method

For the paratha, place the potatoes in a medium-sized bowl and toss with the pickle masala to coat nicely. Set aside for 2-3 hours.

Mash the potatoes with a fork. Add to the whole-wheat flour along with the oil and salt. Make a soft dough and set aside. Divide the dough into 6 portions. Roll out each one into 7-inch disc. Cook on a hot griddle with a little oil, turning on both sides. Allow it to cool.

For the topping, heat the oil in a frying pan, sauté the onions and capsicum until soft. Add the tomatoes, salt and pizza seasoning. Remove from heat and set aside to cool. At the time of serving, take each paratha, spoon the cooled onion-capsicum mixture and spread it evenly. Grate the cheese directly on top and cook under the grill or in a hot tandoor for 3-4 minutes or until the cheese has melted. Cut into wedges, top with the thick yogurt and serve hot.

Makes 6 pizzas

Aloo-Stuffed Thepla

Ingredients

For the thepla

1 cup whole-wheat flour

1 cup millet flour

¼ tsp turmeric powder

1 tsp chilli powder

1 tsp coriander-cumin powder

1 tsp ginger-chilli paste

Salt to taste

1 cup bottle gourd, grated

2 tbsp oil

A pinch of soda bicarbonate

Sour yogurt to bind

Oil for shallow-frying

For the filling

250 gm potatoes, boiled, peeled and mashed

1 tsp dried mango powder

1 tbsp ginger-chilli paste

2 tbsp finely chopped coriander

1 tbsp plain flour

Salt to taste

To serve

Makhana Raita (page 94)

Method

For the thepla, mix together both the flours along with all the dry spices, ginger-chilli paste, salt, bottle gourd, oil and soda bicarbonate. Bind to make a semi-soft dough by adding the yogurt. Do not add water. Divide the dough into 12-14 balls.

For the filling, mix together all the ingredients for the filling in a bowl. Set aside.

Roll out 2 of the dough balls into flat thin discs. Spoon 2-3 tablespoons stuffing mixture, spread evenly on one of the discs and cover with the other. Repeat for the remaining dough.

Shallow-fry the stuffed paratha over medium heat, using little oil. Pour the oil with a small spoon around the edge of the paratha and then slide it off the tawa. Serve with the makhana raita.

Makes 12-14 thepla

Baked Ragda-Pattice

Ingredients

For the ragda

250 gm dried white peas, soaked overnight

A pinch of soda bicarbonate

2-3 tbsp oil

1 medium onion, finely chopped

1 medium tomato, finely chopped

1-2 bay leaves

½ tsp mustard seeds

½ tsp turmeric powder

½ tsp chilli powder

1 tbsp ginger-chilli paste

A few curry leaves

Salt to taste

2 tbsp tamarind pulp

1 tbsp jaggery

½ tsp dried mango powder

Masala for ragda (to be roasted in 1 tbsp oil and powdered)

4 (1-inch) cinnamon sticks

4 cardamoms

4 cloves

5-6 dried round red chillies

5-6 slices dried coconut

½ tsp sesame seeds

½ tsp cumin seeds

½ tsp coriander seeds

½ tsp aniseed

1 tsp peppercorns

1 tsp poppy seeds

For the pattice

1 kg potatoes, boiled, peeled and mashed

2 bread slices, soaked in water

Salt to taste

2 tbsp finely chopped coriander

Juice of 1 lemon

For the potato piping

1 large potato, boiled, peeled and mashed

1-2 tsp butter

1-2 tsp cornflour

Salt to taste

Pepper to taste

1-2 tsp milk

To assemble

½ cup Date and Tamarind Chutney (page 93)

To garnish

Slices of onions, capsicum and tomatoes

To serve

Green Chutney (page 93) or tomato ketchup

Method

For the ragda, cook the peas with soda bicarbonate in the pressure cooker till soft. Set aside.

Heat the oil in a pan and sauté onion until soft. Add the tomato and bay leaves. Add the mustard seeds, powdered masala, turmeric powder, chilli powder, ginger-chilli paste and curry leaves. Fry for 3-4 minutes. Add the boiled peas along with the water they were boiled in, salt, tamarind pulp, jaggery and mango powder. Bring to a boil and simmer till the gravy thickens. Remove from heat and set aside.

For the pattice, mix together the mashed potato with soaked and mashed bread slices, salt, chopped coriander and lemon juice. Make a smooth mixture by mixing with your palms. Divide the mixture into 2 parts and set aside.

For the potato piping, mash the potato and add the butter, cornflour, salt, pepper, and milk. Fill this in a piping bag. Add the extra milk if the mixture feels too dry to pipe.

To assemble, grease an 8 x 10-inch baking dish with oil, and layer half the pattice mixture at the bottom. Spread the cooked ragda over the potato evenly. Spread the date and tamarind chutney and cover with the remaining potato mixture. Apply a little oil if the mixture sticks to your hand while spreading.

Arrange the sliced onions, capsicum and tomatoes on top. Pipe the potato mixture to form a uniform design. Drizzle a little milk and bake in a preheated oven until the top turns golden brown (approx. 20-25 minutes).

Remove and let it cool for 5 minutes. Cut into square pieces and serve hot with the green chutney or tomato ketchup.

Serves 8-10

Buckwheat and Quinoa Dhokla/Khichdi

Ingredients

For the dhokla

½ cup cracked buckwheat, washed and soaked in a little water

½ cup quinoa, washed and soaked in a little water

½ cup sour yogurt

1 tbsp ginger-chilli paste

1 tbsp chopped coriander

2 tbsp ghee + for greasing

Salt to taste

For the khichdi

1 tbsp ghee

½ tsp cumin seeds

1-2 green chillies, chopped

A few curry leaves

1 medium sweet potato, boiled and cut into small cubes

1 recipe Dhokla (recipe above)

2-3 tbsp peanuts, roasted and coarsely ground

1 tbsp sugar

1 tbsp lemon juice

Salt to taste

To garnish

Finely chopped coriander and grated coconut

To serve

Green Chutney (page 93), for the dhokla

Tempered coconut milk, for the khichdi

Method

For the dhokla, rinse the soaked buckwheat and quinoa. Soak in the yogurt for 10 minutes. Add the ginger-chilli paste, coriander, ghee and salt. Mix well. Place the dhokla steamer on heat with water and place a steel ring in the centre. Grease a 10-inch round stainless steel plate with rim (thali) with ghee and pour the prepared mixture onto it. Place the plate on the ring, in boiling water. Cover tightly with the lid. Steam for 10-12 minutes. Remove from heat and set aside to cool slightly. Cut into squares and serve hot with the green chutney.

For the khichdi, heat the ghee in a thick-bottomed pan; add the cumin seeds, green chillies and curry leaves. Cook for 2-3 minutes; add the potato and cook for another 2-3 minutes. Crumble the cooled dhokla and add to the potato. Mix well. Add the peanuts, sugar, lemon juice and salt. Garnish with the coriander and grated coconut. Serve hot with the tempered coconut milk.

Serves 4-6

Cauliflower in Yogurt Sauce

Ingredients

1 kg cauliflower
¾ cup milk
1-inch ginger
3 green chillies, ground into paste
¼ cup grated coconut
3 tsp oil
1 tsp skinless split black gram
2-3 cinnamon sticks
2-3 cloves
A pinch of asafoetida
A few curry leaves
2-3 bay leaves
1 cup beaten yogurt
1 tsp salt

To garnish

Finely chopped coriander and grated coconut

To serve

Paratha or truffle naan

Method

Chop the cauliflower into small pieces. Wash in hot water and place in a pan. Pour the milk over it and cook until milk dries up. Grind together the ginger, green chillies and grated coconut. In another pan, heat the oil; add the split gram and fry until pale golden brown.

Add the cinnamon, cloves, asafoetida, curry leaves and bay leaves. Add the ground paste and fry for 2-3 minutes. Add the yogurt and bring to a boil. Add the cauliflower and salt and mix well. Garnish with the coriander and coconut. Serve hot with the paratha or truffle naan.

Serves 4-6

Cauliflower Rice Pulav

Ingredients

1 medium cauliflower (approx. 4 cups florets)

½ tsp turmeric powder

2 tsp coriander powder

2 tsp garam masala

½ tsp mustard seeds

Pepper to taste

Sea salt to taste

3 tbsp oil

1 tbsp ginger-garlic paste

1 medium onion, diced

1 medium capsicum, diced

1 medium carrot, diced

½ cup French beans, chopped

½ cup shelled green peas

8-10 cherry tomatoes, sliced

¼ cup finely chopped spring onions

To garnish

Chopped coriander and chopped nuts

Method

Grate or chop the cauliflower to resemble rice grains. Mix together all the dry spices and sea salt in a small bowl. Heat a wok and add 1 tablespoon oil and toss in the grated cauliflower. Cook till the cauliflower starts to brown. Add 1 tablespoon oil, then add the ginger-garlic paste, onion, capsicum, carrot, French beans and peas. Cook until the vegetables are soft. Remove from heat and set aside.

In a small pan heat 1 tablespoon oil and roast all the dry spices for 30 seconds. Toss everything back in the wok and add the sliced tomatoes and spring onion. Coat evenly with the spices. Cook for 2-3 minutes. Transfer to a serving dish, garnish with the chopped coriander and nuts. Serve hot.

Serves 4

Curried Corn with Couscous/Rice

Ingredients

For the paste

1 tbsp ghee
1 tbsp coriander seeds
1 tbsp caraway seeds
1 tbsp curry powder
1 tbsp garam masala
1 medium onion, roughly chopped
5-6 dried red chillies
5-6 garlic cloves
1 tsp cumin seeds
1 tsp cloves
1 tsp cinnamon pieces
½ cup freshly grated coconut
Salt to taste

For the curry

2 tbsp ghee
1 tsp cumin seeds
A few curry leaves
A few bay leaves
1 tsp sugar
2-3 medium tomatoes, boiled and puréed
2 large corn on the cob, cut into 1-inch pieces and boiled
2-3 cups medium thin coconut milk

To garnish

Freshly chopped coriander, curry leaves, a few corn kernels

To serve

Couscous or steamed rice

Method

For the paste, heat the ghee in a small pan, roast all the ingredients until fragrant. Remove and set aside to cool. Grind into a smooth paste.

For the curry, heat the ghee in a thick pan, add the cumin seeds, curry leaves and bay leaves. Add the paste and roast until spices change colour. Add the sugar and the tomatoes and roast further for 5 minutes.

Add the boiled corn and mix well. Add the coconut milk and cook further until all the ingredients are incorporated. Arrange the corn pieces stacked up on one side and put dollops of couscous on the other side and garnish with the chopped coriander, curry leaves and corn kernels. Serve warm.

Serves 6

Curried Vegetables Wraps

Ingredients

½ cup finely chopped onion
½ cup finely chopped capsicum
1 tbsp ginger-garlic paste
½ cup finely chopped carrot
1 cup thinly shredded cabbage
1 tbsp curry powder
1 tbsp oil
1 cup mashed potato
¼ cup boiled green peas
Salt to taste
1 tbsp lemon juice
1 tbsp coriander leaves
1 cup grated cheese
8 Buckwheat Wrappers (recipe follows)

To serve

Sour Cream (page 96)

Method

Sauté the onion, capsicum, ginger-garlic paste, carrot, cabbage and curry powder in the oil. Cook on medium heat until vegetables are tender crisp. Remove from heat and add the mashed potato, peas, salt, lemon juice and coriander. Set aside to cool.

Spread ½ cup potato mixture on each wrapper, top with ¼ cup cheese and roll in jellyroll fashion. Press gently to seal. Brush it with a little oil and bake for 10 minutes or till thoroughly heated. Cut into 2 pieces and serve with the sour cream.

Serves 6-8

Buckwheat Wrappers

Mix together ½ cup buckwheat flour with ¼ cup plain flour, ½ tsp salt, ¼ cup finely grated bottle gourd and warm water. Make a soft dough and set aside for 15 minutes. Divide the dough into 8 portions, roll out each one and roast on a dry griddle turning on both sides.

Curry Rissotto

Ingredients

3 tbsp olive oil

2 medium onions, finely chopped

6-8 garlic cloves, chopped

2 cups Arborio rice

1 tbsp curry powder

4 cups warm thin vegetable stock

2 cups coconut milk

1 cup white wine or extra vegetable stock

Salt to taste

Pepper to taste

To garnish

Sliced cherry tomatoes, chopped coriander and grated Parmesan cheese

Method

In a medium-sized pan heat the oil on medium heat. Sauté the onion and garlic until fragrant. Add the rice and curry powder and mix gently. Lower the heat and pour the warm vegetable stock, 1 cup at a time, waiting for it to be absorbed before adding the next cup. In between the warm stock add the coconut milk and wine, little at a time.

Allow the risotto to simmer until all the liquids have been added and absorbed. Add the salt and pepper. Stir time to time to make sure that the rice does not burn. This process should take 25-30 minutes. When the rice is cooked al dente (cooked but firm to bite), transfer to a serving bowl and garnish with the cherry tomatoes, coriander and Parmesan cheese. Serve hot or warm.

Serves 4-6

Dum Aloo Jhalmudi

Ingredients

1 tbsp ghee
2-3 cardamoms
2-3 cloves
2-3 bay leaves
2-3 (2-inch) cinnamon sticks
500 gm small potatoes, boiled and peeled
2 tbsp mustard oil
2 tbsp onion paste
1 tbsp ginger-chilli-garlic paste
1 tsp turmeric powder
1 tsp red chilli powder
1 tbsp garam masala
Salt to taste
1 tsp sugar
3-4 green chilli, slit
4 tbsp milk or cream

To garnish

Jhalmudi and chopped coriander

Method

Heat the ghee in a pan and add the cardamom, cloves, bay leaves and cinnamon. Fry for 1 minute. Add the potatoes, toss and set aside. In another small pan heat the mustard oil, then add the onion paste, ginger-chilli-garlic paste, turmeric powder, chilli powder and garam masala. Fry for 3-4 minutes.

Add this to the potatoes. Add the salt and sugar, mix well, then add the green chillies. Cook for 2 minutes. Add the milk just before removing from heat. Transfer onto a serving platter, and garnish with the jhalmudi and chopped coriander. Serve hot.

Serves 6

Foil Baked Curry and Rice

Ingredients

3 cups cooked rice
1 tbsp oil

For the curry

1 tbsp oil
6-8 shallots, chopped
2 tbsp red chilli-garlic paste
2 tbsp curry powder
2 stems spring onions, cut into 2-inch pieces
½ cup broccoli florets, blanched
½ cup boiled cubed potatoes
½ cup boiled peas
3 cups thin coconut milk

2-3 tbsp tamarind pulp
1 tbsp brown sugar
Salt to taste

Method

For the curry, heat the oil in a pan and fry the shallots and chilli-garlic paste. Add the curry powder and fry for 2-3 minutes. Add the spring onions, broccoli, potatoes and peas. Mix well. Add the coconut milk, tamarind pulp, brown sugar and salt. Bring to a boil and simmer until thick. Set aside.

Toss the cooked rice with the oil. Take a large piece of foil and place it on an oven tray. Spread the rice in an approximately 8-inch disc. Pour curry in the centre, leaving the rice border around. Make a parcel of the foil and place under the grill for 7 minutes. Serve hot.

Serves 6

French Beans Thoran on Appalum

Ingredients

500 gm French beans, cut into small pieces

4-5 shallots, chopped

3-4 green chillies, finely chopped

¼ tsp turmeric powder

Salt to taste

½ cup grated fresh coconut

For the tempering

3 tsp oil

1 tsp mustard seeds

1 tsp split white gram

2-3 dried red chillies

A few curry leaves

A pinch of asafoetida

To garnish

Finely chopped coriander and mulgapodi

To serve

Fried appalum

Method

For the tempering, heat the oil in a thick-bottomed wide pan, add all the tempering ingredients one after the other.

Add the chopped vegetables along with the green chillies, turmeric powder and salt. Cook on high heat for 3-4 minutes. Add the coconut and mix well. Remove from heat and set aside.

To serve, place an appalum on a serving plate, spoon the vegetable and garnish with the chopped coriander and mulgapodi. Serve immediately.

Serves 8

Indian Stir-Fry Bar

Ingredients

For the stir-fry

Oil for stir-frying
250 gm cottage cheese, cut into cubes
250 gm onions, cubed
250 gm green capsicum, cubed
250 gm tomatoes, cubed
250 gm cauliflower florets, blanched
250 gm green peas, blanched
250 gm potatoes, peeled and boiled
250 gm carrots, peeled and boiled
250 gm sweet potatoes, peeled, boiled
250 gm ladies' fingers, chopped into 2-inch pieces
250 gm French beans, chopped into 2-inch pieces
250 gm small brinjals, sliced
250 gm boiled sprouted moong
4-5 paratha of your choice
4-5 roti of your choice
2 medium onions, finely chopped
2 medium tomatoes, finely chopped
3-4 garlic cloves, sliced
1-2 tbsp turmeric powder
Salt to taste
1-2 tbsp chilli powder
1-2 tbsp garam masala
1-2 tbsp chaat masala
1-2 tbsp coriander-cumin powder
Juice of 1 lemon

For the tandoori marinade

2 tbsp tandoori masala
2 tbsp garam masala
2 tbsp chilli powder
1 medium onion, grated
½ cup beaten yogurt
½ cup tomato purée
½ cup chopped coriander
Salt to taste
Pepper to taste
Sugar to taste
Cumin powder to taste

To garnish

Finely chopped coriander

To serve

Paratha, naan, tandoori roti, yogurt, Makhani Gravy (recipe follows) and Spiced Yogurt (page 97)

Method

Mix together all the ingredients for the marinade in a wide bowl.

Option 1

Heat 1-2 tablespoons oil in a frying pan or a wok; add the cottage cheese cubes and stir-fry for 3-4 minutes or until slightly golden. Remove and add to the prepared marinade along with the cubed onions, capsicum and tomatoes.

Allow it to marinate for 2-4 hours. In the same frying pan, add the marinated mixture and cook on medium heat until all the liquid is absorbed. Serve hot with the paratha or naan, a dry dish or serve with the makhani gravy for an elaborate dish.

Option 2

Heat the oil in a wok or frying pan; add 2-3 vegetables of your choice or vegetables like cauliflower, green peas and potatoes. Stir-fry for 2-3 minutes. Add the salt, chilli powder and cumin powder. Mix well. Remove from heat and serve hot with the tandoori roti.

Option 3

Heat the oil in a wok; add 2 tablespoons finely chopped onion, and sliced garlic. Cook until soft. Add 2 tablespoons finely chopped tomato, salt and ladies' fingers. Mix well. Cook until soft. Add chilli powder and cumin powder to taste. Serve hot with the roti and spiced yogurt.

Option 4

Heat 1-2 tablespoons oil in a frying pan; add 2 tablespoons chopped onion and 2 tablespoons chopped tomato. Sauté for 2-3 minutes. Add ½ teaspoon turmeric powder, 1 teaspoon chilli powder, 1 teaspoon garam masala, 1 teaspoon chaat masala and 1 teaspoon coriander-cumin powder. Stir-fry for 2 more minutes.

Make 2 x 2-inch pieces of paratha and add to the mixture in a frying pan. Toss gently to mix. Garnish with the coriander and serve with the spiced yogurt on the side.

Option 5

Heat the oil in a frying pan; add ½ teaspoon each of chilli powder, garam masala, chaat masala, coriander-cumin powder and roast well. Add sprouted moong, salt and lemon juice. Cook for 1-2 minutes. Garnish with the coriander and serve with the yogurt.

Option 6

Heat 1 tablespoon oil in a wok; sauté 3-4 pieces of sliced garlic for 1 minute. Add ½ teaspoon turmeric powder, ½ teaspoon chilli powder, ½ teaspoon garam masala, ½ teaspoon sugar and ½ teaspoon salt. Cook for 1 minute.

Add the sliced eggplant and cook until soft. Garnish with the coriander and serve hot with the roti and spice yogurt.

Serves 8-10

Makhani Gravy

Ingredients

50 gm butter
2 medium onions, finely chopped
2 tbsp chopped garlic
2 tbsp grated ginger
250 gm tomatoes, blanched and chopped
3 tsp red chilli powder
1 tsp garam masala
1 tsp coriander-cumin powder
1 tsp poppy seeds
Salt to taste
½ -¾ cup tomato purée
¼ tsp turmeric powder
¼ tsp clove-cardamom powder
1 bay leaf
2 tbsp cashew nuts
1 tsp dried fenugreek leaves
1 tsp sugar
½ cup fresh cream

To garnish

2-3 tbsp finely chopped coriander

Method

Heat the butter in a pan, sauté the onion, garlic, ginger, tomatoes, chilli powder, garam masala, coriander-cumin powder, poppy seeds, and salt. Add 1½ cups water along with the tomato purée, turmeric powder, clove-cardamom powder, bay leaf and cashew nuts.

Bring this to a boil on low heat until thick, discard the bay leaf. Liquidize once cooled and pass it through a sieve. Add the dried fenugreek leaves, sugar and cream. Garnish with the chopped coriander. Set aside.

Makes 3-4 cups

Makai no Handvo

Ingredients

1½ cups corn niblets, boiled and slightly crushed

2 medium potatoes, boiled and mashed

¼ cup gram flour

1 cup cooked rice

1 cup thick coconut milk

½ tsp turmeric powder

1 tbsp ginger-chilli paste

¼ cup finely chopped coriander

2 tsp powdered sugar

2 tbsp lemon juice

Salt to taste

1 tbsp Eno fruit salt

For the tempering

4 tbsp oil

2 tsp mustard seeds

2 tsp sesame seeds

2-3 round red chillies

A few curry leaves

To serve

Tomato sauce or Green Chutney (page 93)

Method

Mix together all the ingredients, except the fruit salt, in a bowl. When you are ready to bake, add the fruit salt to the mixture, mix well and pour into a 8 x 8 greased baking dish.

For the tempering, heat the oil in a small pan and add the mustard and sesame seeds. When they splutter, add the chillies and curry leaves. Sprinkle this over the vegetable mixture.

Preheat the oven at 200°C/400°F/Gas Mark 6 for 10 minutes. Bake in the pre-heated oven for 25-30 minutes or until the top is golden. Remove and cool slightly. Cut into small square pieces and serve with the tomato sauce or green chutney.

Serves 6-8

Masala Khandvi Pie

Ingredients

1½ cups gram flour, sieved

4½ cups buttermilk (2 cups yogurt + 2½ cups water)

½ tsp turmeric powder

¼ tsp asafoetida

Salt to taste

1½ cups mixed boiled vegetables, diced

1-2 tbsp ginger-chilli paste

½ cup finely chopped onion

½ cup finely chopped tomato

For the tempering

1 tbsp oil

½ tsp mustard seeds

½ tsp sesame seeds

3-4 green chillies, sliced

A pinch of asafoetida

A few curry leaves

To garnish

Finely chopped coriander, grated coconut, fried gram flour crispies

Method

In a heavy-bottomed pan, mix together the gram flour, buttermilk, turmeric powder asafoetida and salt. Churn the mixture with a wooden whisk until lump free. Place the pan on heat and stir continuously. When the mixture begins to get thick, add the remaining ingredients and continue stirring. Cook until the mixture attains a thick consistency. Remove from heat and pour onto a greased 8-inch pie dish. While still hot, smoothen the surface on top and allow it to cool completely.

For the tempering, heat the oil in a small pan, add mustard and sesame seeds, when they splutter, add the chillies, asafoetida and curry leaves. Once it stops to splutter, remove from heat and spread evenly on the set khandvi. Garnish with the coriander, coconut and gram flour crispies and serve cold or room temperature.

Serves 8

Oats and Ragi Dosa

Ingredients

¾ cup oats

¾ cup finger millet flour

¾ cup ready-made dosa batter

Salt to taste

Oil for cooking

To serve

Coconut Chutney (page 92)

Method

Mix together the oats, millet flour and dosa batter in a bowl and set aside for 1-2 hours. Add the salt and adjust the water to make a batter of thin flowing consistency. Heat the dosa griddle to very hot and cool it down a bit by splashing some water on it.

Pour ¼ cup batter and spread with a flat spoon to form a very thin pancake. Drizzle a little oil all over the pancake. Cook until golden and take off the griddle by gently scraping at the bottom of the dosa with a sharp flat spatula.

Serve hot with the coconut chutney.

Serves 6

Palak Paneer Frankie Rolls

Ingredients

6 (5-inch) soft whole-wheat rotis

For the palak paneer filling

1 cup finely chopped spinach
½ cup crumbled cottage cheese
¼ cup whole-wheat flour, sieved
¼ cup gram flour, sieved
1 tbsp rice flour
1 tbsp yogurt
1 tsp sugar
1 tsp chaat masala
1 tsp fennel seeds
½ tsp turmeric powder
½ tsp chilli powder
Salt to taste
Oil for cooking

To serve

Yogurt mixed with Green Chutney (page 93) and sliced onions

Method

For the filling, mix together all the ingredients except the oil, in a medium-sized bowl. Mix well to form a firm mixture. Pull out small part of the mixture and shape into 4 x 1-inch cylindrical rolls.

Heat the oil in a shallow pan and fry them in batches. Place the fried roll in the centre of the roti, roll it up tightly and wrap each frankie roll in foil. Serve with the yogurt mixed with green chutney and sliced onions.

Makes 6 rolls

Paneer Bhurji Kulcha

Ingredients

For the filling

1 tbsp ghee

1 medium onion, finely chopped

1 tbsp ginger-chilli-garlic paste

1 medium tomato, finely chopped

1 tsp chilli powder

1 tsp garam masala

1 tsp salt

2 cups grated cottage cheese

For the kulcha

3 cups plain flour, sieved

1 tsp salt

1 tsp baking powder

1½ tsp dry yeast

1 tsp sugar

2 tbsp ghee or butter

4 tbsp yogurt

To garnish

Finely chopped coriander and chopped green chillies

Method

For the filling, heat the ghee in a small pan, sauté the onion and ginger-chilli-garlic paste together for 2-3 minutes. Add the tomatoes, spices and the salt. Cook for 2-3 minutes and remove from heat. Allow it to cool, then add the cottage cheese and salt. Set aside.

For the kulcha, sieve the flour with salt and baking powder. Place it in a large bowl with a well in the centre and set aside. Mix together in a small bowl, ½ cup lukewarm water with dry yeast and sugar and keep it covered in a warm place for 10 minutes. When frothy, add it to the flour, along with the ghee.

Rub this into the flour with your fingertips to make a soft dough with yogurt, and more water if needed. Keep it covered for 2 hours or until it doubles in volume. Punch down the dough and knead it. Divide it into 8 portions. Roll out each part into a disc, put 2 tablespoons stuffing in each one and close like a ball. Gently press it down and reroll it to form a teardrop shape. Brush it with a little ghee and bake it in the tandoor until black specks appear. Remove and add chopped coriander and green chillies and cook it in the tandoor again for 1 minute. Serve hot.

Makes 8 kulche

Panipuri Crêpes

Ingredients

For the crêpes

50 gm whole-wheat flour
50 gm semolina
1 tbsp sugar or ½ tsp salt
1 tsp baking powder
1 cup milk
4 tbsp butter, melted
Oil for frying

For the filling

½ cup sprouted whole green gram, boiled
½ cup red Bengal gram, boiled
½ cup cubed and boiled potato

For the paste

½ cup coriander leaves
½ cup mint leaves
1 tbsp ginger-chilli paste
1 tsp panipuri masala
1 tsp dried mango powder
Juice of ½ a lemon
A pinch of jaggery
Black salt to taste
Salt to taste

To serve

Sweet and Sour Chutney (page 97)

Method

For the crêpes, sieve together the whole-wheat flour, semolina, sugar or salt and baking powder. Mix this with the milk to make the batter. Add the melted butter and mix. Set aside. Place a thick-bottomed frying pan with 3-inch diameter disc over moderate heat and grease them with butter.

Pour 1 tablespoon batter into the discs and swirl the pan around so that the mixture spreads evenly over the base of the discs. Allow to cook for 3-4 minutes, then turn it over gently with a spatula and cook on the other side. The pan should not be too hot before you pour the batter. Continue until all the mixture is used. Place the prepared crêpes on a large plate lightly greased with butter and cover them with butter paper, until ready to use.

For the filling, mix together all the ingredients in a bowl.

For the paste, grind all the ingredients to a paste. Add this paste to the filling mixture. Set aside.

To assemble and serve, take 1 crêpe and place it on a plate. Spoon 1-2 tablespoons filling mixture on one side of the crêpe and fold the other part over. Repeat for the rest. Place 2 to 3 crêpes on a serving plate and garnish with the sweet and sour chutney.

Serves 6

Pav-Bhaji Biryani

Ingredients

For the rice

2 cups Basmati rice, washed and soaked in water

1 tbsp ghee

Salt to taste

For the bhaji

1 tbsp oil

1 medium onion, finely chopped

1 tbsp red chilli-garlic paste

1 tbsp pav-bhaji masala

Salt to taste

2-3 medium tomatoes, grated

1 cup mixed vegetables, finely chopped and boiled (French beans, carrots, peas, potatoes)

2 tbsp butter

Lemon juice to taste

To garnish

Finely chopped coriander

To serve

Roasted papad and yogurt

Method

For the rice, place 4 cups water in a wide pan and cook the rice with the ghee and salt. Cook until the water is absorbed. Cover and set aside for 10 minutes. Fluff up the rice with a fork. Set aside.

For the bhaji, heat the oil in a frying pan; add the onion and chilli-garlic paste. Fry for 1 minute. Add the pav-bhaji masala and salt along with a little water. Cook until properly roasted and the oil separates from the spices. Add the tomatoes and the boiled vegetables. Mix well. Use the potato masher to mash the vegetables slightly. Remove from heat and add the butter and lemon juice. Mix well.

To assemble, layer 1 cup cooked rice in a tiffin box, top it with ¾ cup prepared bhaji and cover with 1 cup cooked rice. Press gently after every layer. Smoothen the top and close the lid. Garnish with the chopped coriander and serve with the roasted papad and yogurt.

Alternately, you can also mix the prepared bhaji with the rice and toss gently. Pack in individual box and your pav bhaji biryani is ready to go.

Serves 4

Pav-Bhaji Burger

Ingredients

6-8 ladi pav

2-3 tbsp butter

For the patty

1 tbsp oil

1 medium onion, finely chopped

1 medium capsicum, finely chopped

1 medium tomato, finely chopped

1 tbsp red garlic chutney

Salt to taste

1 tbsp pav-bhaji masala

1 cup mixed vegetables, finely chopped and boiled

1 tbsp butter

250 gm potatoes, boiled, peeled and mashed

1 tbsp lemon juice

6-8 cheese slices

Breadcrumbs to roll

Oil for cooking

For the topping and assembling

Red garlic chutney, as required

½ cup finely chopped onion

Hand full of finely chopped coriander

Salt to taste

Chilli powder to taste

To serve

Lemon wedges, finely chopped onion, masala papad

Method

Slit each pav horizontally; apply butter and set aside.

For the patty, heat the oil in a frying pan; sauté the onion and capsicum until soft. Add the tomato, garlic chutney, salt and pav-bhaji masala. Roast until a rich brown colour appears and the oil separates. Sprinkle a little water if the spices stick to the pan. Add the mixed vegetables and butter, and remove from heat. Mix this with the mashed potatoes, add the lemon juice and adjust salt. Shape the potato mixture into balls with a dent in the centre. Place folded cheese slice in the centre. Cover the cheese properly with the potato mixture and shape into patties. Roll them in breadcrumbs. Heat the oil in a frying pan and fry until golden on both sides.

For the topping and assembling of the burger, take a buttered pav, place it on a hot flat pan to heat it through. Brush both the pieces of pav slightly with the garlic chutney. Place the bottom part on the cutting board, place the prepared patty on top, sprinkle with the onion, coriander, salt and chilli powder. Cover with the top part of the pav and serve hot with the lemon wedges, onion, and masala papad.

Makes 6-8 burgers

Left to Right – Aachari Aloo Paratha Pizza (page 56), French Beans Thoran on Appalum (page 68)

Tri-Coloured Dhokla Flan (page 84)

Sarson da Saag Kababs on Corn Tostadas

Ingredients

500 gm fresh mustard leaves, washed
200 gm spinach leaves, washed
2 tbsp ghee
1 tbsp ginger-garlic paste
1 tsp jaggery
Gram flour, as required

For the spice mix (mixed together in a bowl)

1 tsp garam masala
1 tsp cardamom powder
1 tsp cumin powder
1 tsp dried mango powder
1 tsp salt
1 tsp pepper
½ tsp turmeric powder
½ tsp mace powder
½ tsp chilli powder

To garnish

Sweet and Sour Chutney (page 97), white butter, sliced ginger, and spiced popcorn

To serve

4-inch round corn tostada and chilled buttermilk

Method

Drain and chop the mustard and spinach leaves finely. Heat 1 teaspoon ghee in a frying pan, sauté the ginger-garlic paste for 1 minute. Add the washed and chopped leaves and cook until they wilt.

Remove from heat and add the jaggery, spice mix and enough gram flour to be able to bind and shape like a patty. Make 3-inch patties and cook them in batches, on a hot griddle, with a little ghee on both sides of the patties. Keep warm.

To serve, place 1 tostada on a plate, place 1 patty on top and drizzle with the sweet and sour chutney and dot with white butter. Stick the sliced ginger in the centre. Scatter the popcorn around. Serve with a shot of buttermilk.

Serves 6-8

Shahi Pulav with Tomato-Coconut Shorba

Ingredients

For the shahi pulav

2 tbsp ghee

1 cardamom

1 cinnamon stick

1 tbsp cashew nuts, sliced

1 tbsp almonds, sliced

1 tbsp raisins

4 cups cooked Basmati rice

A few saffron threads mixed with 2 tbsp milk

Salt to taste

For the shorba gravy

3 medium tomatoes, roughly chopped

1 medium onion, roughly chopped

1 tsp chopped green chilli

1 tsp grated ginger

1 tsp grated garlic

2 tbsp freshly grated coconut

2 tbsp oil

1 bay leaf

1 black cardamom

1-inch cinnamon stick

3-4 cardamoms

3-4 cloves

3-4 peppercorns

¼ tsp turmeric powder

¼ tsp sugar

½ tsp chilli powder

½ tsp cumin powder

½ tsp garam masala

1 tsp coriander powder

Salt to taste

To garnish

Finely chopped coriander and toasted nuts

Method

For the shahi pulav, heat the ghee in a wide thick-bottomed pan.

Add the cardamom, cinnamon, cashew nuts, almonds and raisins. Fry for 1-2 minutes. Add the rice, saffron-milk mixture and salt. Mix well and set aside.

For the shorba gravy, grind together the tomatoes, onion, green chilli, ginger, garlic and fresh coconut to a paste with 1-2 tablespoon water. Set aside.

Heat the oil in a thick-bottomed pan; add the whole spices and sauté till fragrant. Add the shorba paste and stir well. Then add the turmeric powder, sugar, chilli powder, cumin powder, garam masala and coriander powder. Cook until the oil separates. Add water or vegetable stock and salt.

Cook on low heat for 5-6 minutes until the gravy thickens slightly and has a rich colour. Remove from heat and transfer to a serving bowl. Garnish with the chopped coriander.

To serve, spread and press in the pulav into a ring mould tin and heat slightly. Invert the mould onto a serving plate and place a small bowl in the centre in which you pour the shorba gravy. Garnish with the chopped coriander and some more nuts. Serve hot.

Serves 6

Table Top Mixed Chaat

Ingredients

250 gm mixed fried snack (bhajia/pakodi)
250 gm crisp gram flour snack (gathia, sev)
250 gm snack of your choice (samosa, kachori, dal vada)
½ cup spiced peanuts
½ cup fried channa dal
½ cup masala channa
1 cup boiled chickpeas
1 cup boiled and cubed potato
½ cup finely chopped onion
½ cup finely chopped tomato
½ cup finely chopped unripe mango
Salt to taste
Roasted cumin powder to taste
Chilli powder to taste
Chaat masala to taste
Juice of a lemon, to taste
½ cup Date and Tamarind Chutney (page 93)
½ cup Green Chutney (page 93)
1 cup thick yogurt

To garnish

Finely chopped coriander, fresh pomegranate kernels, fried boondi

Method

Display the first 6 ingredients in individual bowls. Select the preferred snacks from the above mentioned bowls and place them in one large bowl. Add the boiled chickpeas, potatoes, onions, tomatoes, unripe mango, salt, spices, lemon juice and toss to mix.

Add a little of both the chutneys and yogurt. Fill the remaining chutneys and the yogurt in syringes or bottles with nozzles. Place the tossed chaat in the centre of a serving plate, and drizzle with the chutneys and yogurt around it. Garnish with the chopped coriander, pomegranate kernels and boondi. Serve immediately.

Serves 6-8

Tomato Pancakes

Ingredients

½ kg red tomatoes
6-8 shallots, peeled
1 tbsp ginger-chilli paste
1 tbsp red chilli paste
3 cups dosa batter
½ cup semolina
A pinch of asafoetida
Salt to taste
Ghee or oil for cooking
½ cup cottage cheese, crumbled

To serve

Coconut Chutney (page 92)

Method

Blend together the tomatoes, shallots, ginger-chilli and red chilli paste. Place the dosa batter in a large bowl; add the semolina, tomato mixture, asafoetida and salt. The mixture should be of spreading consistency. If it looks thick, add a little water.

Heat a heavy-bottomed griddle and brush it with ghee or oil. Pour 2-3 tablespoons prepared batter and spread evenly. Sprinkle with a little of the crumbled cottage cheese. Cover and cook for 3-4 minutes. When you see the sides turning brown, scrape it with a sharp flat spatula from the griddle and fold over to form a semi-circle. Serve hot with the coconut chutney.

Serves 8-10

Tri-Coloured Dhokla Flan

Ingredients

For the white layer

1 cup ready-made dhokla flour
½ tsp dried fenugreek seeds
½ tsp sugar
1½ cups sour buttermilk, at room temperature
1 tbsp ginger-chilli paste
Salt to taste
Juice of 1 lemon
1 tbsp oil
1 tsp fruit salt

For the green layer

1 cup split green gram, soaked for 6 hours
1 tbsp coriander leaves, finely chopped

1 tbsp ginger-chilli paste
Salt to taste
1 tbsp oil
1 tsp fruit salt
Juice of ½ lemon

For the yellow layer

1 cup gram flour, sieved
1½ tbsp semolina
3 tbsp oil
Salt to taste
3 tsp sugar
½ tsp citric acid
1 tsp fruit salt
1 tsp soda bicarbonate
Juice of ½ lemon

For the tempering

2 tbsp oil
1 tsp mustard seeds
1 tsp sesame seeds
½ tsp asafoetida
3-4 green chillies, chopped

To garnish

Chopped coriander and coconut

To serve

Green Chutney (page 93)

Method

For the white layer, mix together the dhokla flour, fenugreek seeds, sugar and buttermilk in a large bowl. Cover and place the bowl in a closed oven or cupboard overnight to ferment. Next morning, ensure that the batter has fermented and risen. Mix well and add the ginger-garlic paste and salt. Check if the batter is of dropping consistency; if not add a little warm water to make it thinner.

Boil the water in a steamer. Grease an 8-inch ring mould tin with the oil and place it over the boiling water. In a small bowl, mix together the lemon juice, oil, 2 tablespoons hot water and fruit salt. As soon as it starts frothing, mix it in the batter with an upward movement, and pour the batter into the prepared tin. Steam covered for 4-5 minutes. Subsequently, prepare the green layer.

For the green layer, coarsely grind the green gram along with the chopped coriander and water to a paste. The batter should not be too thick or thin. Mix together the green gram batter, ginger-chilli paste, salt, 1 tablespoon oil and the fruit salt mixed with lemon juice. Mix the batter lightly in a circular movement, until all the ingredients are incorporated properly. Immediately pour this over the half-steamed white layer in the steamer. While this is steaming, make the yellow layer.

For the yellow layer, mix together the gram flour and semolina. Add 2 tablespoons oil, salt, sugar and half of ¾ cup water. Set aside. In a small bowl, mix together the remaining water, citric acid, 1 tablespoon oil, fruit salt, soda bicarbonate and lemon juice and add this to the flour mixture. Mix the batter lightly in a circular movement, until all the ingredients are incorporated properly. Immediately pour this onto the half-steamed green layer in the steamer. Cover tightly and steam for 15 minutes. Remove from the steamer and allow it to cool for 10 minutes. Unmould the tin on a serving plate.

For the tempering, in a small pan, heat the oil, add the mustard seeds and sesame seeds, when they splutter add the asafoetida, green chillies and curry leaves. Allow it to splutter for 1 minute. Add 1 tablespoon water and pour this over the steamed dhokla flan. Garnish with the chopped coriander and coconut. Serve hot. Serve hot with the green chutney.

Serves 6-8

Uttapam Duo

Ingredients

2 cups ready-made dosa batter

1 cup skinless split black gram, soaked for 4 hours and ground to a paste

1 tbsp ginger-chilli paste

½ cup finely chopped onion

½ cup finely chopped tomato

2 tbsp finely chopped coriander

Salt to taste

Oil for cooking

To serve

Coconut Chutney (page 92)

Method

Place both the batters in separate bowls. Add enough water to make a batter of dropping consistency. Divide the remaining ingredients, except the oil, into 2 parts and add to each batter.

Heat a non-stick or thick-bottomed frying pan; brush with a little oil. Place a 3-4-inch circular steel ring on the pan and pour in the dosa batter to make a thick pancake. Slowly lift up the ring and place it on the other side of the pan and pour the split gram batter in the same manner.

Cover and allow both the pancakes to cook. When almost done, take a 2-inch round pastry cutter and cut out discs from both the pancakes. Remove the small discs and place the dosa batter discs on to split gram batter discs and vice-versa. Press gently and try and merge both discs. Gently flip over the pancake discs and cook on the other side. Serve hot with the coconut chutney.

Serves 8

Vegetable Handvo

Ingredients

1½ cups mixed vegetables (cauliflower, peas and carrots), chopped and boiled

2 medium potatoes, cubed and boiled

¼ cup gram flour

1 cup maize flour

1½ cups thick coconut milk

½ tsp turmeric powder

1 tbsp ginger-chilli paste

¼ cup finely chopped coriander

2 tsp powdered sugar

2 tbsp lemon juice

Salt to taste

1 tbsp fruit salt

For the tempering

4 tbsp oil

2 tsp mustard seeds

2 tsp sesame seeds

2-3 dried round red chillies

A few curry leaves

To serve

Tomato sauce or chutney

Method

Grease an 8 x 10-inch baking dish with oil. Mix together all the ingredients except the fruit salt in a bowl. When you are ready to bake, add the fruit salt to the mixture and pour it into the baking dish.

For the tempering, heat the oil in a small pan and add the mustard and sesame seeds. When they splutter, add the chillies and curry leaves. Sprinkle the tempering over the vegetable mixture.

Bake in a hot oven at 240°C/475°F/Gas Mark 9 for 25-30 minutes or until the top is golden. Remove and cool slightly. Cut into small square pieces and serve with the tomato sauce or chutney.

Serves 6-8

Vegetable Kurma

Ingredients

1 medium carrot, peeled and cut into 1-inch pieces

10-12 French beans, trimmed and cut into 1-inch pieces

¼ cup cauliflower florets

½ cup fresh green peas

1 medium turnip, peeled and cut into 1-inch pieces

2 tbsp oil

1 bay leaf

1 star anise

1 tsp mustard seeds

1 medium onion, finely chopped

A few curry leaves

2 tsp red chilli powder

2 tsp garam masala

Salt to taste

1 medium tomato, quartered

For the paste

½ cup fresh grated coconut

1 tsp fennel seeds

½ tsp cumin seeds

8-10 cashew nuts

1 tbsp poppy seeds

1-inch ginger

5-6 garlic cloves

2 cardamoms

2 (1-inch) cinnamon sticks

2 cloves

¼ tsp turmeric powder

To garnish

Finely chopped coriander and grated coconut

To serve

Lemon flavoured rice vermicelli, appum and mango pickle

Method

Place the carrots, French beans, cauliflower, peas and turnip in a sieve over a pan of boiling water and steam them for 10-15 minutes. Set aside.

Grind together all the ingredients for the paste, using a little water, to attain a smooth consistency and set aside. Heat the oil in a wide pan or a wok. Add the bay leaf, star anise and sauté until fragrant. Add the mustard seeds and let them splutter. Add the onions, curry leaves and sauté until the onions turns translucent. Add the red chilli powder, garam masala, salt and mix well. Add the ground paste and enough water to attain the consistency you prefer the kurma to be, mix well and cook on low heat. Allow the mixture to come to a boil.

Add the par boiled vegetables, quartered tomato, give it a quick stir, check the consistency of the kurma and add more water if necessary. Cover the pan with a lid leaving a small gap for the steam to escape and let the kurma cook over medium low heat for 7-10 minutes. When the gravy has thickened considerably, remove from heat, garnish with the chopped coriander and coconut. Serve hot on the bed of lemon flavoured rice vermicelli. Serve the appum and mango pickle as an accompaniment.

Serves 8

Vegetable Samosa Pie

Ingredients

For the pastry crust

¾ cup plain flour

¾ cup whole-wheat flour

½ tsp salt

2 tbsp hot oil + for brushing pastry

For the filling

2 tbsp oil

1 tsp caraway seeds

1 medium onion, finely chopped

3 garlic cloves, crushed

1 tbsp ginger-chilli paste

1 tbsp garam masala

1-2 tsp dried mango powder

1-2 tsp red chilli powder

1-2 tsp sugar

5 medium potatoes, boiled and cut into small cubes

1 cup shelled green peas, boiled

Salt to taste

Milk for brushing pastry

To serve

Cucumber Raita (page 95)

Method

For the pastry crust, mix both the flours together in a bowl, add the salt and toss. Make a well in the centre and rub in the oil. Slowly add in cold water, 1 tablespoon at a time, until the dough holds together. Shape into a ball, cover with damp cloth and set aside.

For the filling, heat the oil in a frying pan, add the caraway seeds, when they splutter, add the onions and garlic. Cook until soft. Add the ginger-chilli paste, garam masala, dried mango powder, chilli powder and sugar. Cook for 2-3 minutes. Sprinkle a little water if the spices stick to the pan. Add the potatoes, peas, and salt. Mix well and set aside to cool.

Divide the dough in 2 parts (three-quarters and one-quarter). Roll out the three-quarters part into an 11-inch disc and press this into a 9-inch pie dish. Press gently with your palm to make sure no air bubble remain. Lightly brush the dough with milk to avoid drying.

Transfer the potato mixture over the crust and spread it evenly to level the top surface. Roll out the remaining dough into a 9-inch disc and press it over the potato mixture. Mark an 'x' in the centre with a sharp knife to vent steam. Brush the top with the oil and bake in a hot oven at 350°F/180°C/Gas Mark 4, for 35-40 minutes. Remove from the oven and cool slightly before serving. Serve with the cucumber raita.

Serves 6-8

Wild Mushroom and Truffle Kulcha

Ingredients

For the filling

1 tbsp oil

1 medium onion, thinly sliced

2 cups sliced wild mushrooms

Salt to taste

For the kulcha

3 cups plain flour, sieved

1 tsp salt

1 tsp baking powder

1½ tsp dry yeast

1 tsp sugar

4 tbsp yogurt

2 tbsp ghee or butter

To garnish

Truffle oil

Method

For the filling, heat the oil in a small pan; sauté the onion and mushrooms for 2-3 minutes and remove from heat. Allow it to cool and add the salt. Set aside.

For the kulcha, sieve the flour with the salt and baking powder. Place it in a large bowl with a well in the centre and set aside. Mix together in a small bowl, ½ cup lukewarm water with dry yeast and sugar and keep it covered in a warm place for 10 minutes. When frothy, add it to the flour along with the ghee. Rub this into the flour with your fingertips to make a soft dough with yogurt and more water, if needed. Keep it covered for 2 hours or until it doubles in volume.

Punch down the dough and knead it. Divide into 8 portions. Roll out each portion into a disc, place 2 tablespoons stuffing in each and close like a ball. Gently press it down and reroll it to form a teardrop shape or round disc. Brush it with a little ghee and bake it in the tandoor till black specks appear. Remove and drizzle with truffle oil, and place in the tandoor again for 1 minute. Cut into 4 pieces and serve hot.

Makes 8 kulche

Accompaniments

Coconut Chutney

Ingredients

1 cup grated coconut
1 chopped green chilli
1-inch ginger
1 tablespoon coriander leaves
1 tablespoon sugar
1 tablespoon skinless split Bengal gram, soaked
½ cup thick yogurt
Salt to taste

Method

Mix together all the ingredients except the yogurt and salt. Grind in the grinder and add ½ cup thick yogurt and salt to taste.

Makes 1 cup

Cucumber and Wasabi Raita

Ingredients

250 gm cucumber, peeled and chopped or grated
Salt to taste
3-4 tbsp peanuts, skinned, roasted and coarsely ground
1 tsp sugar
Juice of 1 lemon
1 cup thick yogurt
1 tsp wasabi paste

To garnish

Finely chopped coriander

Method

To the cucumber, apply the salt and set aside for ½ an hour. Rinse off the excess water from the cucumber and place it in a bowl. Add the remaining ingredients and mix well. Garnish with the chopped coriander and chill until ready to serve.

Serves 4-6

Date and Tamarind Chutney

Ingredients

200 gm seedless dates
A walnut-sized ball of tamarind
Salt to taste
Chilli powder to taste

Method

Cook the dates, tamarind, 2 cups water, salt and chilli powder in the pressure cooker till the pressure is released 2-3 times (2-3 whistles). Cool. Process the mixture in a blender until smooth and pass through a strainer. If you find the chutney a little thin, boil for 5-10 minutes until thick. Use as required.

Makes 1½ cup

Green Chutney

Ingredients

2 cups roughly chopped coriander leaves
½ cup fresh mint leaves
2-3 chopped green chillies
1-inch ginger
½ teaspoon cumin seeds
1 teaspoon sugar
1 tablespoon roasted split Bengal gram
Juice of 1 lemon
A pinch of asafoetida

Method

Grind together all the ingredients with a little water to make a smooth paste. Store in the refrigerator.

Makes 1 cup

Khajoor aur Mirchi ka Aachar

Ingredients

250 gm whole dates, seeded and cut into cubes
6-7 dried red chillies
1 cup brown vinegar
½ cup grated jaggery
1½-inch ginger, peeled and chopped
1 garlic clove, crushed (optional)
2 green chillies, chopped
1 tbsp split mustard seeds
1 tbsp tamarind pulp
1 tsp poppy seeds, soaked in water
2 tbsp raisins
A few curry leaves
A pinch of nutmeg powder
Salt to taste

To serve

Paratha or ghee rice

Method

Wash and drain the dates. Grind the red chillies with vinegar to a smooth paste and add the jaggery, mix well. Set aside. Transfer this mixture to a pan and add the remaining ingredients and gently heat the mixture until they are well incorporated. Do not boil the mixture. Cover with a tight lid and set aside for 1-2 days. Serve with the paratha or ghee rice.

Makes 2 cups of pickle

Makhana Raita

Ingredients

3 cups yogurt, beaten
½ cup fresh cream
50 gm puffed lotus seeds
2 cups milk
1 tbsp ghee
1 tbsp raisins
1 tbsp sunflower seeds
Salt to taste
Sugar to taste

To garnish

Finely chopped coriander

To serve

Paratha

Method

Mix together the yogurt and cream; strain and place in a refrigerator to chill overnight. Discard the hard black flakes in the lotus seeds and boil in milk till tender. Strain and set aside.

Heat the ghee in a wok and fry the raisins and sunflower seeds. Remove from heat and set aside. Remove the yogurt mixture from the refrigerator and add the boiled and cooled lotus seeds, raisins, sunflower seeds, salt, and sugar, and mix well. Garnish with the coriander and chill. Serve with the paratha.

Makes 3 cups

Raita Bar

1. **Vegetable Raita:** To 1 cup chilled yogurt add, ¼ cup chopped cucumber, ¼ cup chopped tomato, ¼ cup chopped onion, ¼ cup chopped coriander, salt to taste, chaat masala to taste, roasted cumin powder to taste, and chilli powder to taste. Mix well.

2. **Boondi Raita:** To 2 cups yogurt add, 250 gm boondi, salt to taste, chaat masala to taste, roasted cumin powder to taste, chilli powder to taste. Mix well. Garnish with chopped coriander.

3. **Grapes and Walnut Raita:** To 2 cups chilled yogurt add, 25-30 chopped green grapes, ¼ cup chopped walnuts, 1 tablespoon chopped mint leaves, 2 teaspoons roasted cumin powder, salt to taste, sugar to taste, and red chilli powder to taste. Mix well.

4. **Bottle gourd/Pumpkin Raita:** To 2 cups yogurt add, 250 gm peeled, grated and steamed bottle gourd/pumpkin, 1 chopped green chilli, salt and sugar to taste. Make the tempering with 1 tablespoon ghee, ½ teaspoon cumin seeds, a pinch of asafoetida, and curry leaves. Add to the yogurt. Garnish with finely chopped coriander.

5. **Cucumber Raita:** To 2 cups yogurt add, 250 gm grated cucumber, 1 teaspoon kashundi mustard, 1 tsp sugar and salt to taste, 2 tablespoons chopped mint, 2 tablespoons chopped coriander, 2 tablespoons grated coconut and 2 tablespoons roasted and chopped peanuts. Mix well.

Some more combinations:

- Grated carrot raita with tempering
- Steamed and chopped beetroot raita
- Steamed and mashed pink yam raita
- Spinach and dates raita
- Boiled potato and mustard raita
- Apple/pineapple or strawberry raita
- Fried onion raita
- Sautéed brinjal raita with chopped dill

Serves 4-6

Red Salsa

Ingredients

4 medium tomatoes, coarsely chopped
1 medium onion, chopped
3-4 garlic cloves
1 tablespoon red chilli paste
1 tablespoon vinegar
1 tablespoon chopped fresh coriander
2 tablespoons finely chopped jalapeño chillies
1 teaspoon salt
1 teaspoon taco seasoning mix
A large pinch of dried oregano

Method

Place all the ingredients in a blender jar. Blend to make a sauce but take care not to purée it.

Makes 1 cup

Sour Cream

Ingredients

1 cup fresh cream
¼ teaspoon yogurt
1-2 tablespoons lemon juice
1 tablespoon finely chopped chives
2-3 crushed garlic cloves (optional)
Salt to taste

Method

Heat the cream in a small pan until it begins to boil. Remove from heat and set aside till lukewarm. Transfer the cream into a bowl, add the yogurt and mix well. Cover and set aside in a closed cupboard overnight. Remove and beat until smooth. Add the lemon juice, chives, crushed garlic and salt to taste. Mix well. Cover and chill for at least 1 hour before serving.

Makes 1 cup

Indian Stir-Fry Bar (page 69)

Raita Bar (page 95)

Clockwise – Nutberry Bars (page 108), Yogurt Ice Cream with Saffron and Pistachios (page 113), Strawberry Barfi (page 112)

Gulab Jamun Cheesecake (page 101)

Spiced Yogurt

Ingredients

1 cup thick yogurt
½ teaspoon salt
½ teaspoon sugar
½ teaspoon cumin powder
½ teaspoon chilli powder
1 tbsp chopped coriander
1 teaspoon oil from any pickle (optional)

Method

Mix together all the ingredients. In addition, you may add the oil from any pickle for an extra tangy flavour.

Makes 1 cup

Sweet and Sour Chutney

Ingredients

200 gm jaggery
A walnut-sized ball of tamarind
Salt to taste
Chilli powder to taste

Method

In a thick pan mix together jaggery, tamarind, 1 cup water, salt and chilli powder to taste. Cook until the jaggery has melted. Remove from heat and set aside to cool. Transfer to a liquidizer jar and blend until smooth and pass it through a sieve. If you find the chutney a little thin, boil for 5-10 minutes until thick. Use as required.

Makes 1½ cups

Tomato Chutney

Ingredients

1 tablespoon oil
1 finely chopped onion
4 medium tomatoes, chopped
1 tablespoon sesame seeds
1 tablespoon chopped peanuts
1 teaspoon cumin powder
1 tablespoon red chilli paste
1 tablespoon jaggery
Salt to taste

Method

Heat the oil and fry the onion. Add the tomatoes along with the sesame seeds, peanuts, cumin powder, red chilli paste, jaggery and salt to taste. Remove from heat, cool and grind to a paste.

Makes 1 cup

Sweets and Desserts

Chenna-Stuffed Khajoor

Ingredients

14 large seedless dates
100 gm soft cottage cheese/chenna
1-2 tbsp icing sugar
2 tbsp whipped cream
14 toasted whole almonds
2-3 tbsp toasted walnuts

Method

Slit the dates from the centre vertically. In a small bowl mix together the crumbled cottage cheese, and icing sugar. Mix well. Fold in the whipped cream. Fill this mixture in a piping bag and pipe into the slit dates till a little of the mixture oozes out. Press 2 almonds or 2-3 pieces of broken walnuts and chill for 30 minutes.

Makes 14 stuffed dates

Flavoured Yogurt with Toppings

Ingredients

1 litre chilled yogurt, naturally set in individual cups (You will require 6-8 cups depending on the size)

Toppings

- **Mango, cinnamon and pistachio nuts**

  Place 1 sliced Alphonso mango in an oven-proof dish, sprinkle with ½ teaspoon cinnamon powder. Place under the grill for 2-3 minutes and remove from oven. Spoon this mixture warm or at room temperature over the chilled yogurt and garnish with ½ cup toasted and chopped pistachio nuts.

- **Lemon, almonds and poppy seeds**

  Gently fold in the juice of 2 lemons into the yogurt and garnish with ½ cup slivered and toasted almonds and 2 teaspoons poppy seeds.

- **Almonds, crystallized ginger, orange juice, honey**

  Top the yogurt with ½ cup toasted and chopped almonds; 2-3 tablespoons chopped crystallized ginger, 2 tbsp orange juice, 1 tsp orange rind and 1-2 tablespoons honey.

- **Honey, almond and apricots/figs/dates**

  Fold 3 tablespoons honey into the yogurt and top it with ½ cup chopped and toasted almonds and ½ cup chopped apricots/figs/dates.

Serves 6-8

Gulab Jamun Cheesecake

Ingredients

For the base

200 gm digestive biscuit
50 gm melted butter
¼ cup powdered sugar

For the cheesecake

200 gm Philadelphia cream cheese
100 gm condensed milk
100 gm whipping cream
1 tsp rose water (optional)
1 tsp lemon juice
8-10 small gulab jamuns

To garnish

Slivered pistachios, saffron, rose petals and gold dust

Method

For the base, process the biscuits in a blender to crumble them, or alternately you could break the biscuits up on a greaseproof paper by covering the paper with another piece and firmly roll a rolling pin to and fro until the biscuits become crumbs. Melt the butter in a pan and add biscuit crumbs and sugar. Mix well. Remove from heat and line the base and sides of a 9-inch or 10-inch loose bottom cake tin with the biscuit crumbs and press it with the back of your hand to spread evenly and set aside to cool.

For the cheesecake, process the cream cheese and condensed milk in a blender and empty into a large bowl. Beat the cream until thick and add to the cheese mixture and gently fold in the rose water along with lemon juice. Mix well. Pour half the mixture over the prepared and lined tin. Cover and chill in the refrigerator for 20 minutes. Remove from the fridge and arrange gulab jamuns at regular interval. Pour in the remaining mixture and place in the freezer to set. Remove from the tin and onto a serving plate and garnish with the slivered pistachios, saffron, rose petals, and gold dust.

Serves 6-8

Honey-Laced Baskets with Rose Ice Cream

Ingredients

For the ice cream

500 gm vanilla ice cream

2 tbsp rose syrup

¼ cup chopped nuts

For the baskets

⅓ cup melted butter

4 tbsp sugar

2 tbsp honey

⅔ cup plain flour

1 tbsp grated lemon rind

½ tsp powdered cardamom

To garnish

Rose petals and honey

Method

For the ice cream, mix together the vanilla ice cream, rose syrup, and chopped nuts. Transfer to a tin or airtight box and freeze it overnight until set.

For the baskets, in a medium-sized pan mix together the butter, sugar and honey and heat gently. Stir continuously until the sugar melts. Remove from heat and cool slightly. Mix the flour, lemon rind and cardamom. Add this to the butter mixture and mix well. Place the mixture in the freezer for about 30 minutes.

Divide the mixture into 10 portions and roll into discs. Place these on an inverted deep muffin mould or shallow tart case and bake in a hot oven at 180°C/350°F/Gas Mark 4 for 10-12 minutes until golden brown. Remove from the oven and cool slightly. Remove from the mould and store in an airtight container. To serve, place each basket in an appropriate stemmed glass or bowl and scoop ice cream into it. Garnish with the rose petals and drizzle with honey. Serve at once.

Makes 10

Kalakand Petit Fours

Ingredients

250 gm ready-made kalakand

For the pastry

½ cup powdered sugar

½ cup unsalted butter, at room temperature

¼ tsp nutmeg powder

¼ tsp cardamom powder

¾ cup plain flour

¼ tsp baking powder

A pinch of salt

¼ cup powdered pistachios

For the glaze

300 gm castor sugar

A pinch of cream of tartar
or soda bicarbonate

100 gm icing sugar

1 tbsp fresh cream (optional)

Powdered saffron (optional)

To garnish

Slivered almonds and saffron threads

Method

For the pastry, preheat the oven to 150°C/300°F/Gas Mark 2 for 10 minutes. In a mixing bowl, combine the powdered sugar (little at a time) with the softened butter until the mixture is light and creamy. Add the nutmeg powder and cardamom powder and mix well. In a separate bowl, sift plain flour with baking powder and salt. Add the powdered pistachio. Combine the flour mixture (little at a time) with the butter mixture to form a soft dough. Wrap dough in plastic wrap and let it rest for 15-20 minutes. Knead the dough once again and roll it out in a large rectangular sheet to fit a 12 x 8-inch tin. Bake on the middle rack of the oven for 20-25 minutes, Remove from the oven and quickly make marking with a sharp knife to measure 1 x 1½-inch pieces. Allow the cookies to cool for 5 minutes before transferring to a cooling rack to cool completely. Store in air-tight container.

For the glaze, mix together castor sugar and 200 ml water. Bring to a boil and add the cream of tartar or soda bicarbonate. Continue boiling until it forms a thick syrup. Remove from heat and add the icing sugar. Mix well. Cool slightly and add the cream and saffron (if using). Use immediately to cover the pastry or cake.

To assemble, place the cooling rack that has equal-sized tray placed underneath. Place a few cookies at a time, top with the same size kalakand pieces and cover with another cookie to seal tightly. Pour the prepared glaze over it to cover the whole piece. The tray underneath will collect the spilled glaze so that you can reuse it. Repeat for the remaining cookies. Garnish with the slivered almonds and saffron threads. Set aside till completely set.

Makes 25 pieces

Khajoor and Badam Samosa

Ingredients

20 samosa patti or wonton wrappers

¼ cup milk

Oil for deep-frying

For the filling

2-3 tbsp toasted sesame seeds

½ cup finely chopped dates

½ cup brown sugar

2-3 tbsp chopped almonds

1 tbsp butter

To garnish

2 tbsp powdered sugar

1 tbsp cinnamon powder

To serve

Vanilla ice cream

Method

For the filling, slightly crush the sesame seeds and mix them with the dates, sugar, almonds and butter. Set aside.

Cut the square wonton wrapper into 2 diagonally, to form a triangle. Shape each triangle like a cone, sealing the edge with a little milk. Place 1 teaspoon filling in the centre of a cone and close with a flap. Repeat this for the rest of the wrappers. Set aside to dry for a few minutes.

Deep-fry in oil until golden. Drain on a kitchen paper. Sprinkle a little of the sugar mixed with cinnamon powder on each one and serve hot with the vanilla ice cream.

Makes 20 wontons/samose

Khajoor Halwa

Ingredients

1 cup finely chopped dates

½ cup milk

¾ cup sugar

¾ cup ghee

½ cup chopped cashew nuts

To garnish

Slivered pistachios and almonds, edible gold foil

Method

In a heavy-bottomed pan, mix together the dates, milk and sugar and cook on medium heat. Add the ghee when the mixture comes to a boil. Then add ¼ cup cashew nuts. Cook on low heat till the mixture is almost dry and halwa is formed. Remove from heat and add the remaining cashew nuts. Transfer to a serving dish. Garnish with the pistachio and almonds and gold foil. Serve hot.

Serves 6

Khajoor ki Kheer

Ingredients

1 litre milk

1 tbsp uncooked rice, washed

1 tsp ghee

125 gm rock sugar, crushed

½ tsp each saffron powder

½ tsp cardamom powder

½ tsp nutmeg powder

¼ cup chopped dates

2 tbsp almonds, blanched and sliced

Method

Boil the milk in a pan. Rub the rice with the ghee and add to the milk. Boil till thick and then add the sugar and boil again. The milk should reduce in quantity by a third. Add the saffron powder, cardamom powder and nutmeg powder. Remove from heat and add the dates and almonds. Serve hot or cold.

Serves 4

Lemon Lassi Sorbet

Ingredients

2 cups thick yogurt, churned and chilled
1 cup chilled water or ice cubes
½-¾ cup powdered sugar
Juice of 1 lemon
Mould of your choice

To garnish
A few mint leaves

Method

Blend all the ingredients together in a blender until smooth. Transfer to a metal box and freeze over night or at least for 6 hours. Remove from the freezer and blend once again to remove icicles, if any. Pour into individual moulds or back into the box and freeze for 4-6 hours. Remove and scoop with ice cream spoons into small bowls or stemmed glasses, garnish with the mint and serve immediately.

Serves 6

Mango Barfi in Pistachio Cups

Ingredients

For the barfi
250 gm Alphonso mango pulp
250 gm sugar
1 tbsp ghee
250 gm khoya/mawa

For the pistachio cups
250 gm shelled pistachios
200 gm sugar
A pinch of cardamom powder
1 tbsp ghee
1 tbsp arrowroot flour

To garnish
Slivered almonds

Method

For the barfi, mix the mango pulp and sugar together in a heavy-bottomed pan. Stir until the sugar melts. Cook on low heat for 5-10 minutes. Remove from heat and set aside. Heat the ghee in a frying pan and fry the khoya on low heat until slightly golden. Add to the mango mixture. Return the pan to heat and cook gently, stirring continuously, until thick. Remove from heat and set aside.

For the pistachio cups, place the pistachios in hot water for 5-10 minutes and peel. Pat dry and powder them in a grinder. Heat the sugar and 100 ml water in a pan until dissolved. Remove from heat and add the cardamom powder and powdered pistachios. Mix well. Heat the ghee in a small frying pan and add the pistachio mixture and arrowroot and cook on low heat until thick. Remove and refrigerate this mixture until completely cold. Divide the pistachio mixture into 30 portions and shape into balls first and then into small bowls. Arrange on a serving tray and place 1 tablespoon mango barfi mixture in each one. Garnish with the almonds and chill until ready to serve.

Makes 30 cups

Mango Panna Cotta

Ingredients

1½ tsp agar-agar powder

1 cup milk

1¼ cups cooking cream

⅔ cup powdered sugar

2 medium Alphonso mangoes, peeled and puréed

To garnish

1 medium mango, chopped

Method

Soak the agar-agar powder in ⅓ cup water for 10 minute, stirring from time to time. Bring to a boil until thick and keep warm. In a medium-sized pan, heat the milk, cream and sugar. Bring to a gentle boil. Remove from heat and add the agar-agar mixture in a thin stream.

Make sure both the liquids are hot at this point. Mix well until well incorporated. Set aside to cool slightly. Add the mango pulp and mix really well to get a smooth mixture. Divide this amongst 4-6 individual bowls and set in the freezer for 4-6 hours. Garnish with the chopped mango and serve chilled.

Serves 6

Nutberry Bars

Ingredients

1 cup finely chopped seedless dates
1 cup finely chopped dried figs
¼ cup milk
¼ cup finely chopped cashew nuts
¼ cup finely chopped almonds
¼ cup finely chopped walnuts
¼ cup finely chopped pistachios
1 tbsp ghee
¼ tsp cinnamon powder

Method

Blend the dates and figs with the milk until smooth. Roast all the nuts until golden, crisp and releases aroma. Set aside to cool. Line an 8-inch square pan with foil and set aside.

Heat the ghee in a frying pan and sauté the blended paste until it changes colour and is well cooked. Add the cinnamon powder and keep stirring from time to time until the mixture leaves the sides of the pan. Add the roasted nuts and mix well into the date mixture. Transfer to the prepared pan and smoothen the top. Allow this to rest until the mixture cools completely and slightly firm. Cut into equal squares and store in airtight container.

Makes 20 bars

Nutty Mawa Fudge

Ingredients

50 gm butter
400 gm sweetened condensed milk
2 cups milk powder
½ cup coarsely chopped nuts (almonds and pistachios)
½ tsp powdered saffron mixed with 1 tsp milk
1 tsp cardamom powder

To garnish

Gold and silver dust

Method

For the mawa, melt the butter in glass bowl and heat it in microwave for 30 seconds. Remove and add the condensed milk and milk powder little at a time and continue mixing. Return to the microwave and cook for 2-3 minutes, removing and mixing after every 1 minute. The mixture should leave sides of the bowl. Allow it to cool.

Add the nuts, saffron liquid and cardamom. Either make small cookie-like shapes or you can spread on a cookie sheet and smoothen the sides. Cut into square, rectangular or diamond shaped pieces. Garnish with the gold or silver dust. Chill for 30 minutes in the refrigerator to set. Serve at room temperature.

You can store this in an airtight container, in the refrigerator for a week.

Makes 30-40 pieces

Roasted Almond Ice Cream

Ingredients

400 gm sweetened condensed milk

400 ml fresh cream

¾ cup toasted and chopped almonds

½ tsp vanilla essence

Method

Whisk together all the ingredients till well mixed. Transfer to an airtight plastic box or tin with a lid and freeze it overnight. Alternately, churn in an ice cream machine until set and then transfer to an airtight box and freeze.

Serves 6

Rose Panna Cotta

Ingredients

1 tsp agar-agar powder

2 cups heavy cream (you can use half & half)

2 cups whole milk

½ cup sugar

½ piece vanilla bean, slit in half lengthwise or ½ tsp vanilla essence

¼ cup rose syrup or rose water

To garnish

Edible rose petals

Method

In a small pan, add 1 cup water and the agar-agar powder. Stir and allow the agar-agar to soak for about 10-15 minutes. Bring to a gentle boil on medium high heat. Let it simmer on low heat and stir continuously for about 5 minutes, or until the agar-agar has completely dissolved. Remove from heat and set aside.

In a medium-sized pan, combine the heavy cream with the milk and sugar, on medium heat. Stir well until the sugar has completely dissolved. Then add the entire vanilla bean. Bring to a gentle simmer, cover and remove from heat. Let it stand for at least 15-20 minutes. Then discard the vanilla bean, stir in the agar-agar mixture and then slowly whisk it into the hot cream and milk mixture. Stir well to combine and add in the rose syrup. Stir well and pour into greased oven-safe ramekins, dividing the mixture equally.

Chill in the refrigerator for at least 4-6 hours or longer. To unmold and serve, carefully dip the bottom of each ramekin in a small bowl of hot water for just a minute or so. Then run a small paring knife around the inner edge of the ramekin. Place a small serving plate upside down over the top of the ramekin and carefully invert the ramekin onto the serving plate. Now gently shake the ramekin so that the panna cotta easily slides out onto the serving plate. Garnish with the edible rose petals and serve chilled.

Serves 8

Saffron and Pistachio Soufflé

Ingredients

2 cups milk
5 tbsp sugar
6 tbsp custard powder
2 tsp powdered saffron
1 tsp cardamom powder
2½ tbsp gelatin
3 tbsp powdered sugar
300 gm whipping cream
5 tbsp icing sugar
1 tsp vanilla essence
3 tbsp slivered pistachios

To garnish

Powdered pistachio

Method

Combine the milk and sugar in a pan and heat. Dissolve the custard powder in a little cold milk separately. Add this to the hot milk, stir until thick. Remove from heat and cool. Add the powdered saffron and cardamom powder. Mix the gelatin and powdered sugar in a small pan with 1 cup cold water and cook over medium heat stirring continuously. Cook until it turns transparent and begins to boil. Remove from heat and place the pan over a bowl of ice and beat until it resembles cream.

Whip the whipping cream along with the icing sugar, little at a time until soft peaks form. Set aside ½ cup cream for garnishing. Place a big bowl on ice. Add the cooled custard, cream, vanilla essence, slivered pistachios and beaten gelatin.

Stir often, scraping the sides until the soufflé becomes thick. Pour into a serving bowl and chill for at least 4 hours. Garnish with the reserved whipped cream and pistachio and serve chilled.

Serves 6

Strawberry Barfi

Ingredients

100 gm cottage cheese
200 gm sweetened condensed milk
125 ml strawberry pulp
½ tsp cardamom powder
½ tsp ghee

To garnish

10-12 sliced pistachios,
almonds and chopped strawberries

Method

Mix together the grated cottage cheese and condensed milk in a pan. Place on low heat, stirring continuously so that the mixture does not stick to the pan and it begins to thicken. When the mixture leaves the sides of the pan and clumps together, remove from heat and set aside to cool. Do not overcook, as the barfi will become dense and chewy. Add the strawberry pulp and cardamom powder; mix well. Spread the barfi mixture evenly in a tray greased with ghee. Garnish with the chopped nuts and strawberries and then cut into small squares. Serve at room temperature or refrigerate them.

Makes 16 pieces

Sugarcane Sorbet

Ingredients

1 litre sugarcane juice
1 tsp ginger juice
1 tsp lemon juice
1 cup vanilla ice cream
1 medium melon

Method

Blend all the three juices and vanilla ice cream in a blender. Pour into an ice cream container and freeze for 2-3 hours. Remove from the freezer and blend again. Freeze the blended mixture again for 3-4 hours or overnight.

Cut the melon in half and scoop out the flesh. Use the flesh in another recipe. Chill the melon shell. Scoop the sorbet and fill it into the halved melon and serve.

Serves 4-6

Sutarfeni Delight

Ingredients

1 cup cottage cheese, grated

½ cup icing sugar, sieved

1 tsp cornflour

½ cup fruit of your choice, freshly chopped (pineapple, orange, mango) and chopped mixed dried fruit

250 gm x 2 discs white or saffron-flavoured sutarfeni

¼ cup sugar syrup

To garnish

A few rose petals and slices of fruit

Method

In a medium-sized bowl, mix together the cottage cheese, icing sugar and cornflour. Add the finely chopped fruit. Place 1 sutarfeni disc on a lightly greased baking tray and heat slightly, in a moderate oven, just until a little crisp. Remove from the oven and cool slightly. Place the sutarfeni on a serving dish and evenly spread the cottage cheese mixture over it.Make the other sutarfeni slightly crisp in the oven and place it over the cottage cheese mixture. Pour the sugar syrup over the sutarfeni, making sure it does not trickle out of the sides. Garnish with the rose petals and fruit slices. Cut it into triangles and serve at room temperature or cold.

Serves 6-8

Yogurt Ice Cream with Saffron and Pistachios

Ingredients

400 gm thick yogurt, chilled

½ cup whipping cream

3-4 tbsp powdered sugar

¼ tsp powdered saffron

¼ cup chopped pistachios

To garnish

Sliced pistachios and saffron

Method

Place the yogurt in a sieve to drain out the water, if any. Strain the yogurt to a smooth and creamy consistency. Whip the cream with the sugar until soft peaks are formed. Fold in the cream into the yogurt very gently. Fold in the saffron and pistachios. Transfer this mixture to an airtight box and place in the freezer for 6 hours or more. Shift the box from the freezer to the fridge 2 hours before serving. Garnish with the sliced pistachios and saffron and serve chilled.

Serves 4

Glossary of Terms

Appalum	South Indian style crisp rice crackers
Barfi	Fudge-like Indian sweet
Bhaji	Vegetable dish
Bharta	Roasted and mashed vegetable, like brinjal
Bhurji	Scrambled
Biryani	Mixed spiced rice dish
Boondi	Crisp gram flour droplets
Chaat	Savoury snack made with a variety of ingredients, served hot or cold
Chaat masala	Tangy dry spice mix
Chawli	Dried black eyed beans
Chenna	Soft cottage cheese used to make sweets
Churi	Crumbled
Curry leaves	Meethe neem ka pataa/Kadi patta
Dabeli masala	Special spice mix used for dabeli
Dahi bhalle	Lentil balls marinated in yogurt
Dal	Split pulses
Dhokla	Steamed rice and lentil cakes
Dosa	Crisp lentil and rice pancakes
Garam masala	Indian spice mix
Halwa	Indian dessert
Handvo	Baked savoury cake
Jhalmudi	Bengali-style puffed rice snack
Jiralu	Indian spice mix used as a taste-maker
Kabuli chana	chickpeas
Kachori	Fried spicy lentil dumplings
Kala-khatta	Black sweet and sour sugar syrup
Kashundi mustard	Bengali-style mustard sauce
Khandvi	Gram flour rolls
Kheer	Indian dessert made with rice and milk
Khichdi	Savoury porridge of rice and lentils
Kokum saar	Coconut milk flavoured with juice of Garcinia Indica
Kulcha	Type of Indian flat bread
Kurma	Vegetable gravy dish

Ladi pav	Indian sour dough bread
Lassi	Sweet yogurt-based drink
Malai	Cream that rises to the top of the milk when boiled and cooled
Masala	Spice
Mawa	Reduced milk
Misal rasa	Spiced liquid used for sprouted lentils
Moong papad	Thin green lentil wafers
Mulgapudi powder	South Indian spice powder made from lentils and chillies
Pani puri	Indian snack which is a combination of crisp semolina puffs with spiced water
Pav-bhaji masala	Spice mixture used to prepare pav-bhaji, a popular Mumbai snack
Pulav	Lightly tempered aromatic Indian rice dish
Puri	Puffed or crisp Indian bread
Ragda	Medley of pulses in spicy gravy
Raita	Thick yogurt with vegetables, or boondi or with various other ingredients
Rasam	South Indian style spiced lentil water
Saag	Vegetable dish
Samosa	Fried pastry with triangles with a variety of filling options
Shahi	Royal
Sherbet	Flavoured syrup
Shorba	Soup or Broth
Suterfeni	Indian sweet made from rice flour vermicelli
Tandoor	Indian clay oven
Tandoori masala	Spice mix used while barbecuing or grilling ingredients
Thepla	Gujarati-style flat bread, spiced with various ingredients
Thoran	Vegetable cooked in South Indian style and garnished with coconut
Tikki	Small patty
Tokri	Basket
Udad papad	Thin wafers made of skinless split black gram
Vada	Fried dumplings
Zatar	Thyme-based Lebanese spice

Glossary

English	Hindi
Almonds	Badam
Amaranth	Rajgira
Asafoetida	Hing
Beetroot	Chukandar
Bengal gram, split	Chane ki dal
Black gram, skinless, split	Dhuli udad dal
Black gram, split	Chilkewali urad dal
Bottle gourd	Lauki/doodhi
Brinjal	Baigan
Capsicum	Shimla mirch
Caraway seeds	Shahi jeera
Cardamom	Elaichi
Cashew nuts	Kaju
Cinnamon	Dalchini
Corn kernels	Makai ke dane
Cottage cheese	Paneer
Cumin seeds	Jeera
Dates	Khajoor
Finger millet	Ragi
Gram flour	Besan

English	Hindi
Green gram, skinless split	Dhuli moong dal
Green gram, sprouted whole	Ankurit moong
Green mustard leaves	Sarson
Green peas	Matar
Jaggery	Gud
Kidney beans	Rajma
Mustard	Rai
Peanuts	Moongphali
Pistachio	Pista
Plain flour	Maida
Potatoes	Aloo
Puffed lotus seeds	Makhana
Saffron	Kesar
Semolina	Rawa/sooji
Sesame seeds	Til
Turmeric	Haldi
Turnip	Shalgam
Whole-wheat flour	Gehun ka atta
Yogurt	Dahi